Fantasy Treehouse Art & Architecture

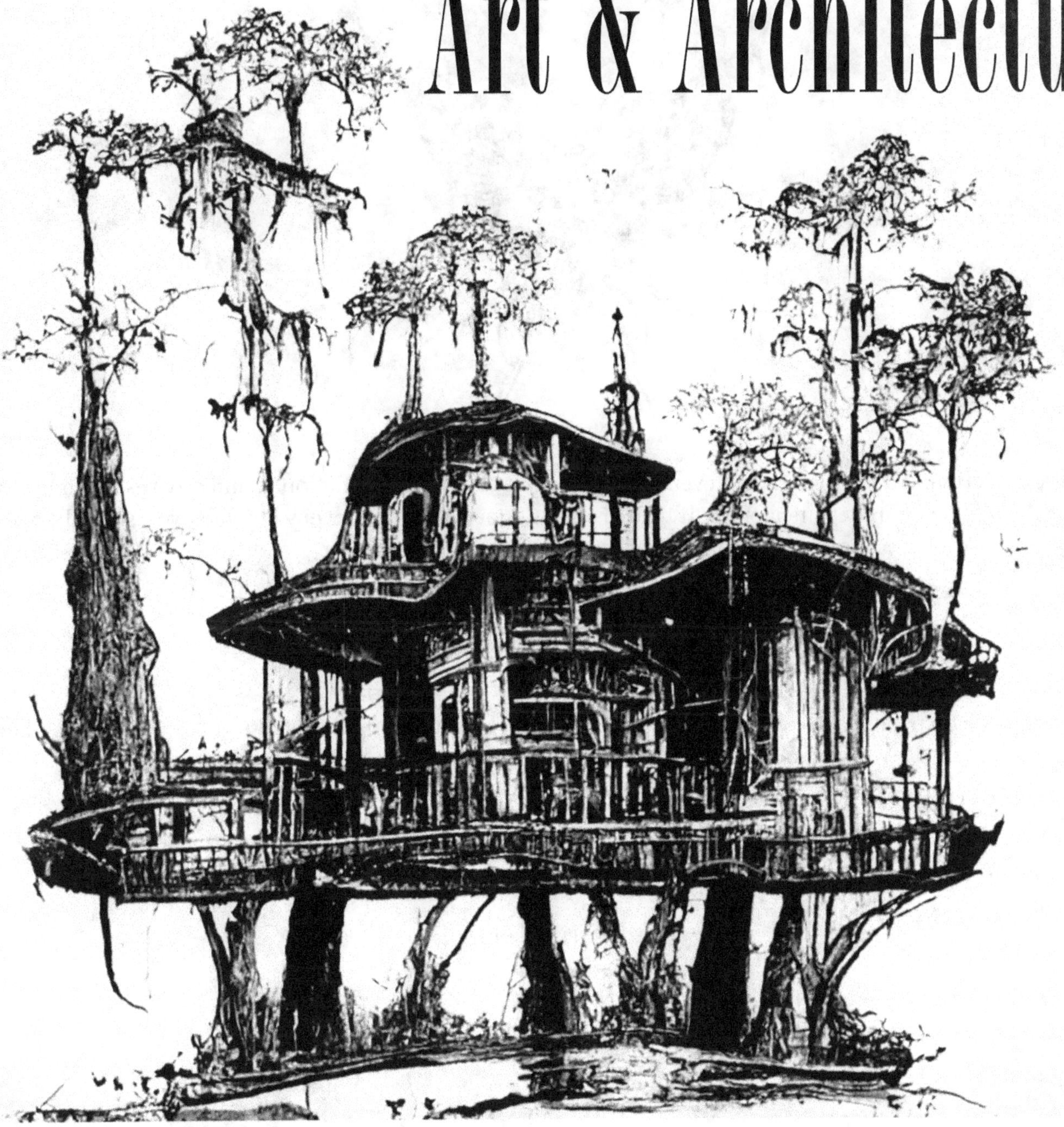

A Forested Flight of Fancy

Dedicated to my mother, Kathleen, who draws houses and taught me how, too.

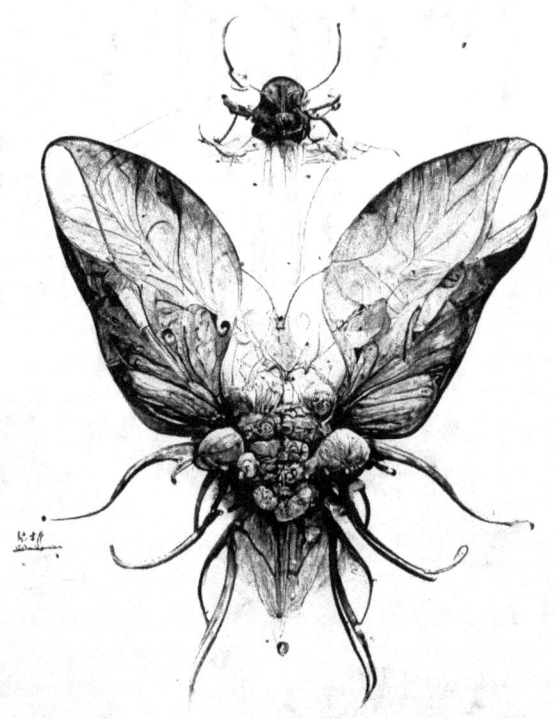

This is a work of fiction. All characters and events portrayed in this work are fictional, and any resemblance to real people or incidents is purely coincidental. If you are seeing faeries in your every day life, you should either see your doctor, or start writing down their stories.

Copyright 2022 by Sanderley Studios

All other rights reserved

Please do not copy or distribute any part of this material as-is. The artist humbly thanks you for respecting her work, and for sharing your colored pages as you desire.

Illustrations and text by Cedar Sanderson

Images pulled from the quantum dimension with the assistance of the artificial intelligence, MidJourney.

www.cedarwrites.com

The dog barked, once, and I knew from her tone the mailman had come. I hurried to the door, and when it swung open there, ignominiously on the porch along with sundry other boxes, was the package I had been waiting for. I picked it up from the steps, warm from the Texas sun, and hurried inside with my prize.

My fingers trembled slightly as I slid my penknife through the carefully taped, barely-visible seams.

At last!

I held in my hands the sketchbooks of *Mme. K.* I cannot reveal her full name at this time, but the exquisite nature of her work brought me to impulsively begin the project, perhaps, of a lifetime. In your hands you hold the first chapter of that... her drawings, with a few notes that may be translated into English by your humble scribe.

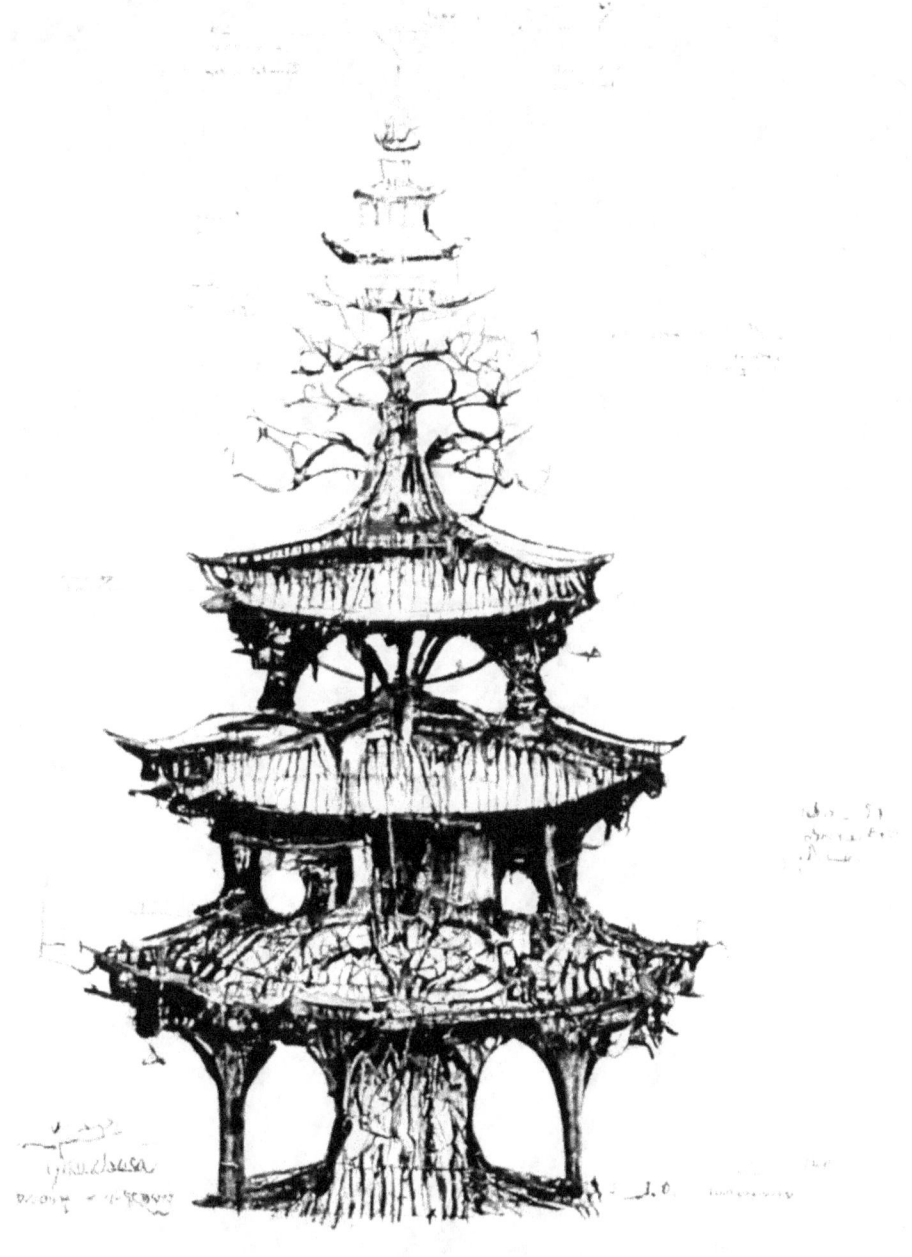

I've been called a tree hugger, but this is a whole new level of embracing the forest. Domiciles woven around, into, and through the trees fill each sketch.

Colors from her sketchbook are fleeting and do not survive the printing process. You may add your own with colored pencils, and bring these pages to life again.

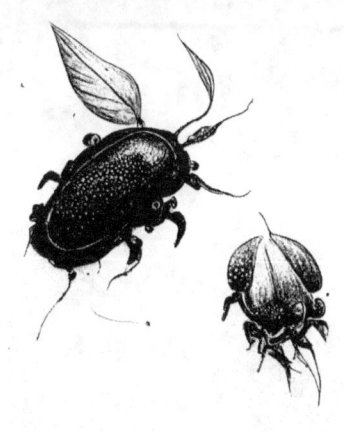

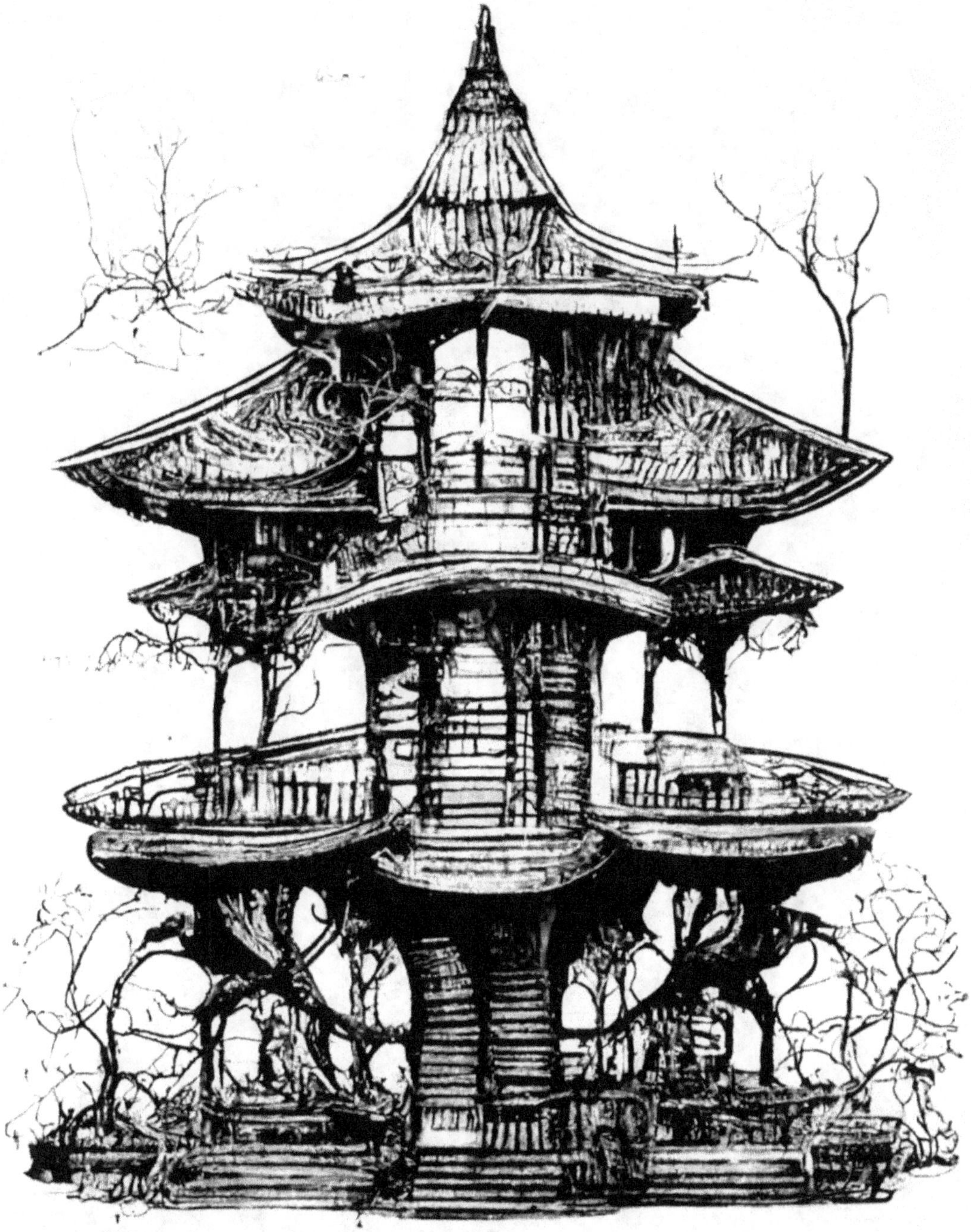

𝓜𝓶𝓮 𝓚. seems to have an especial affinity for the flora and fauna of her environs, and I often wonder what the scale is for some of her sketches. Are they outsized, or to scale with the houses?

A clever use of the lower areas for storage, while the upper living levels are perhaps safer. From what, I wonder?

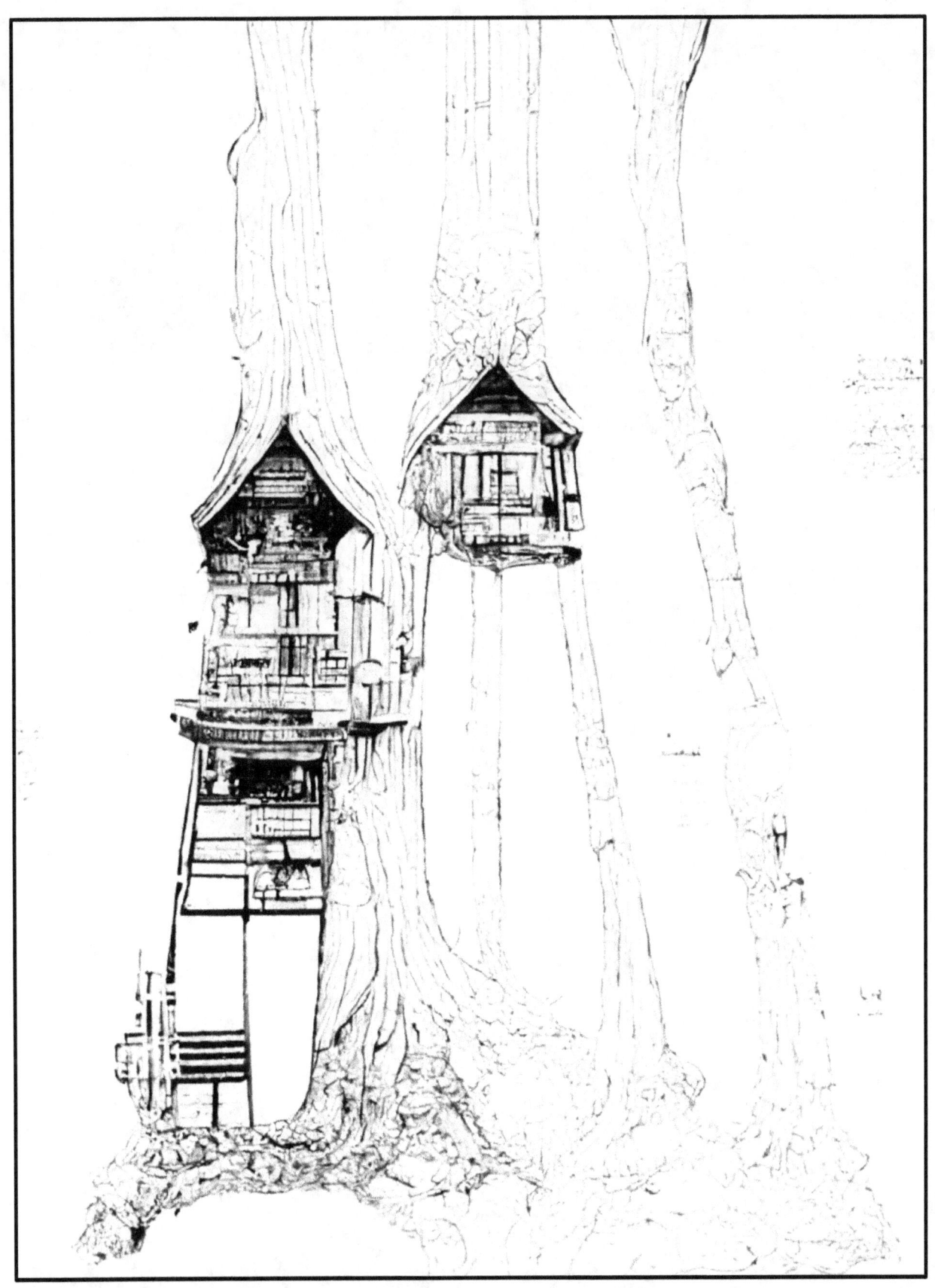

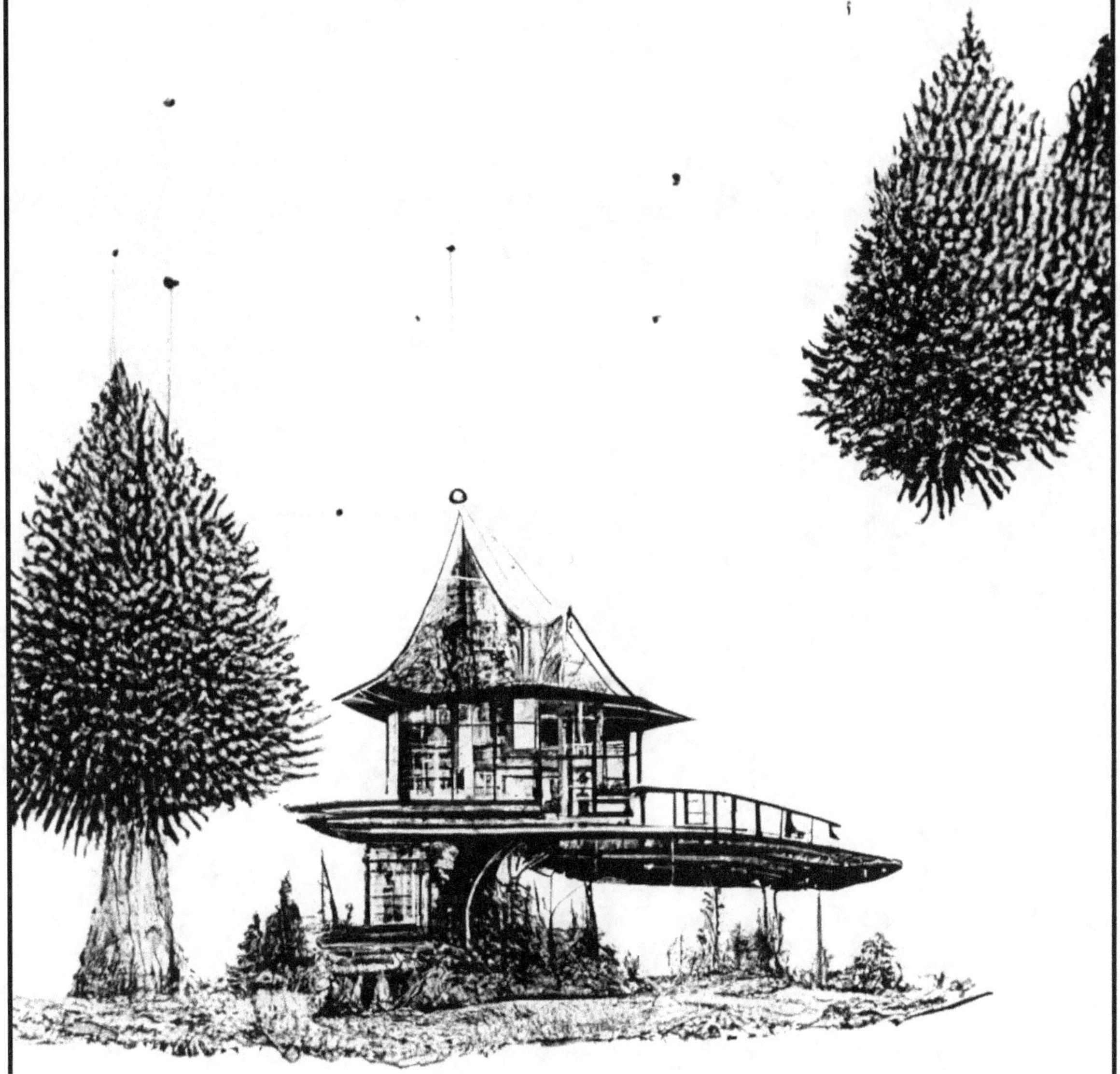

Not all the treehouses are small, although this one seems to be. If they are raising families in these, then everyone spends most of their time out-of-doors!

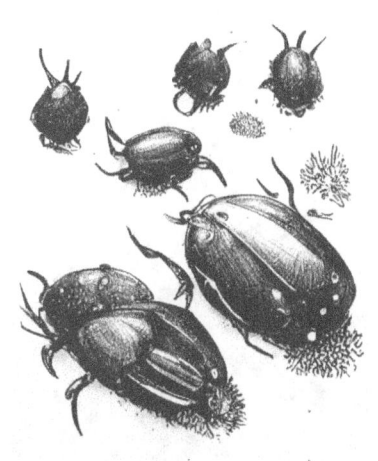

Bits of beetle carapace, leftover from a feast. I wonder what... or who... ate heartily here!

Her notes indicate that she has taken special care here to include the root systems that anchor both the trees and dwellings. They are hidden underground, but she has used her artistic license to indicate the utility of this building style.

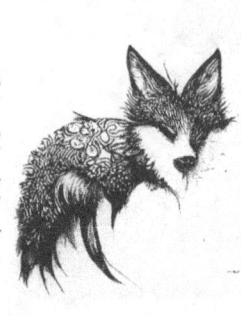

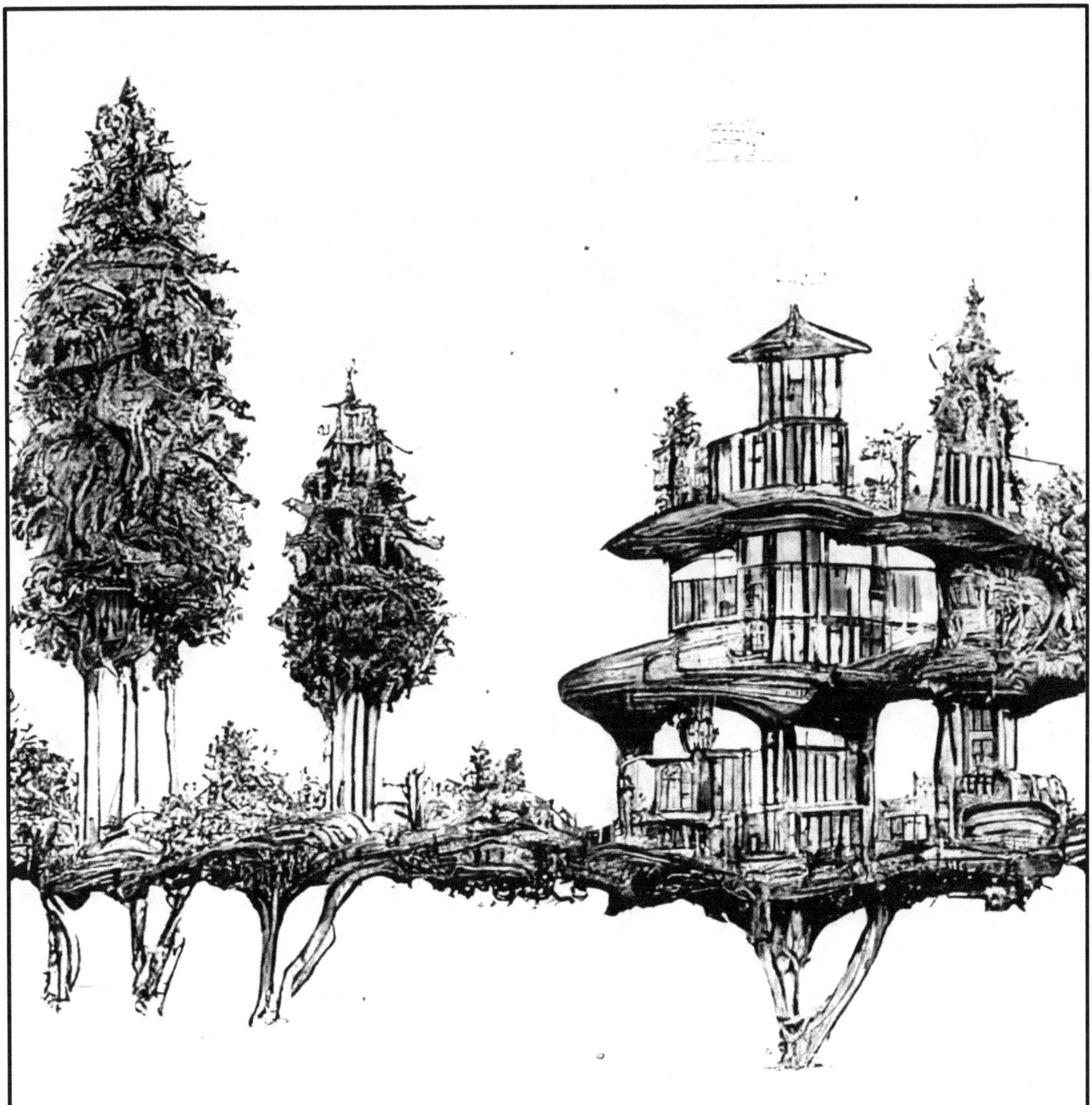

Again, Mme K is showing the cutaway of a structure to illustrate design and engineering for strength, or as her notes call it 'long-life joys' (below her sketch).

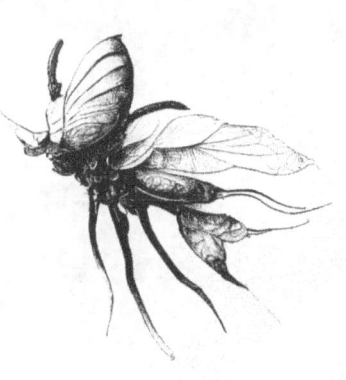

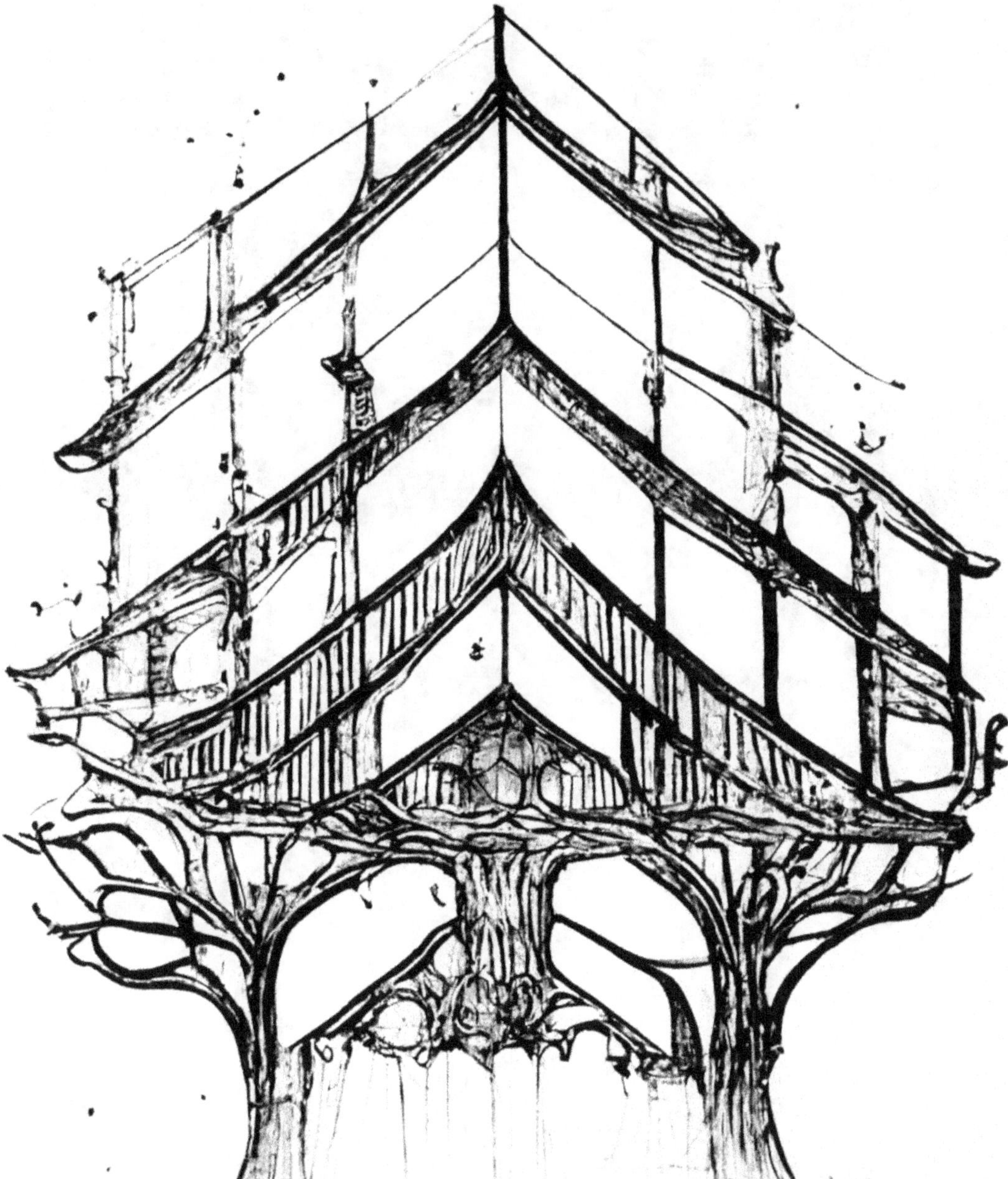

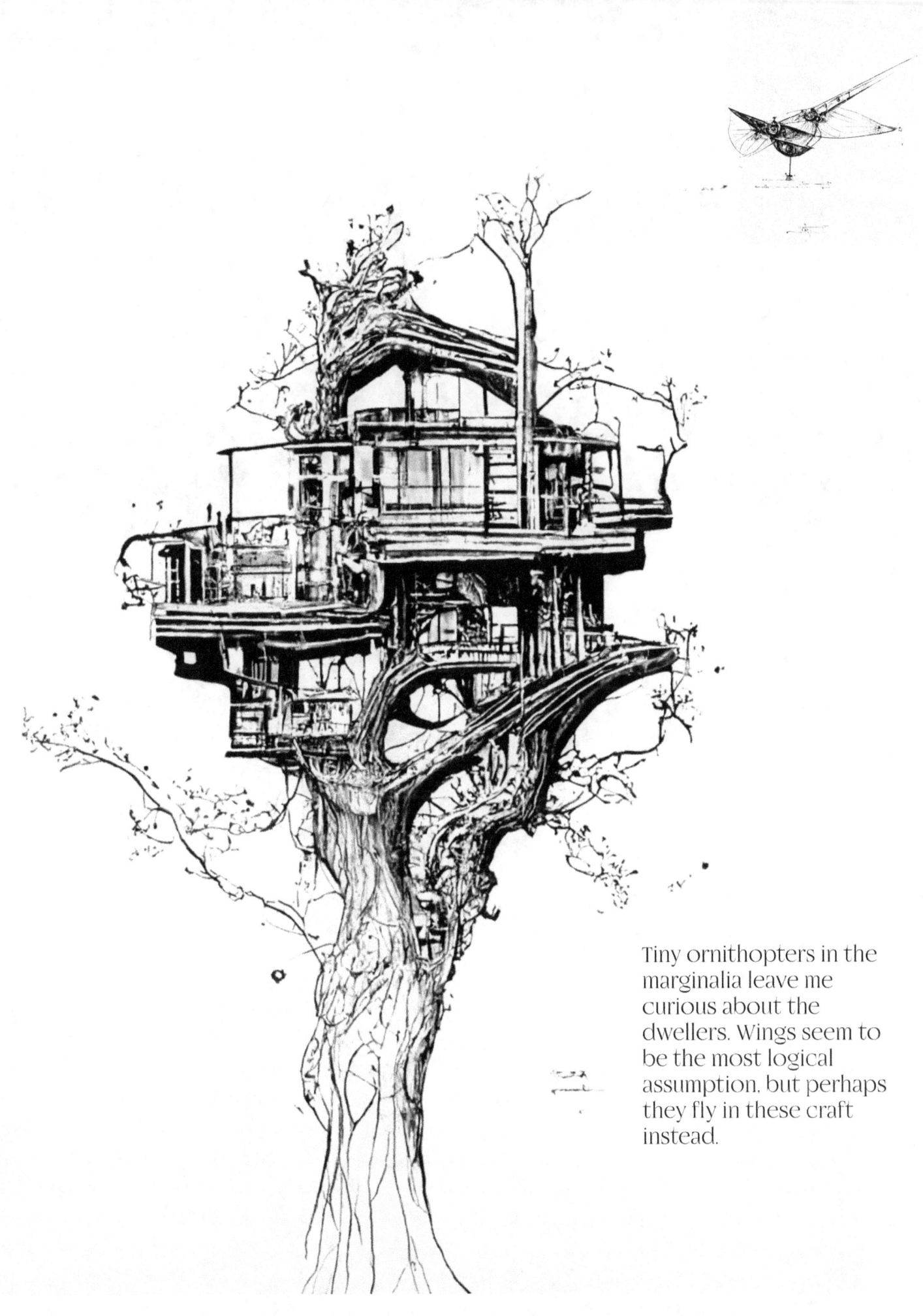

Tiny ornithopters in the marginalia leave me curious about the dwellers. Wings seem to be the most logical assumption, but perhaps they fly in these craft instead.

One wonders if the builders here took the liberty of grafting and training, with methods we might use on bonsai, to fit the tree to the house.

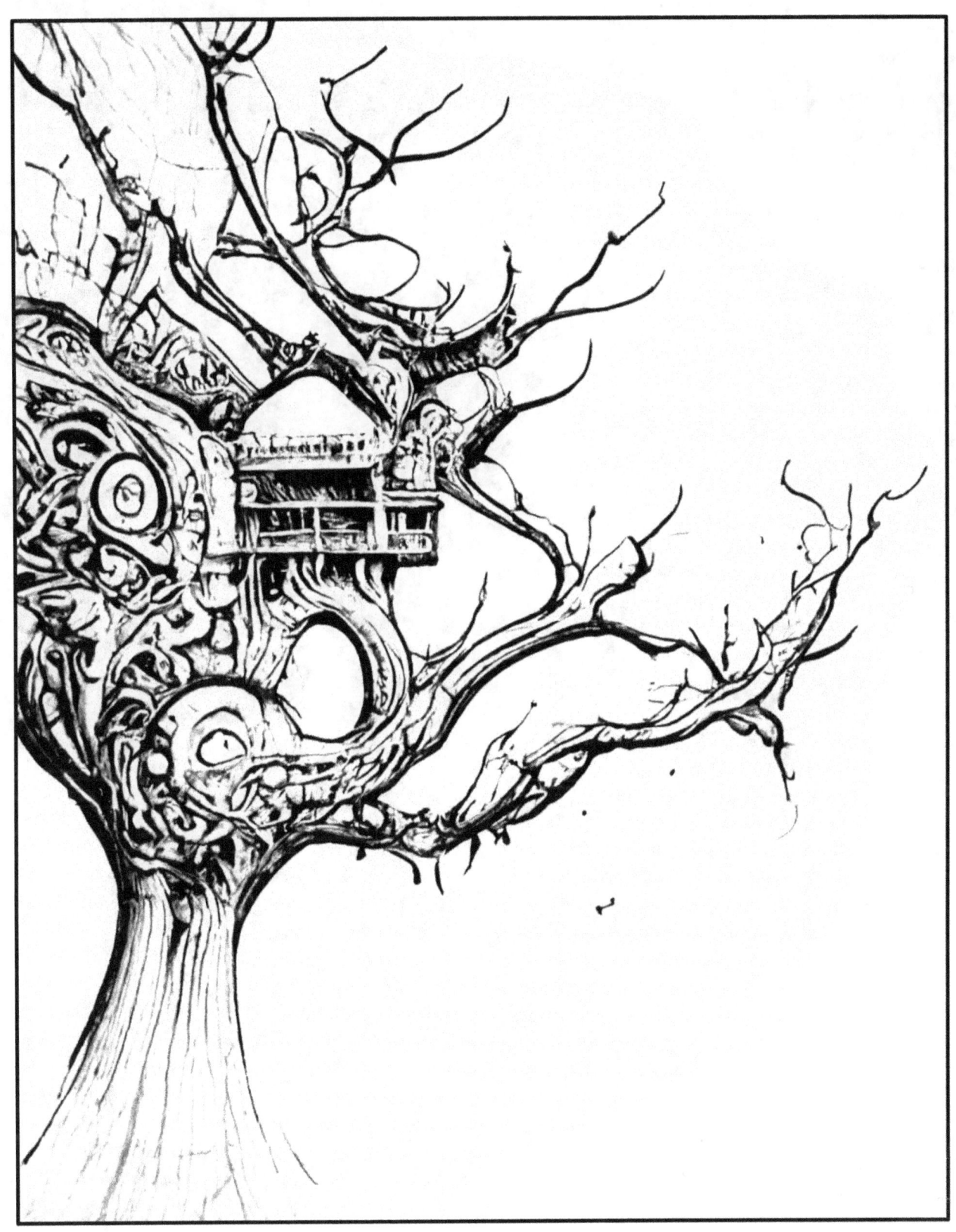

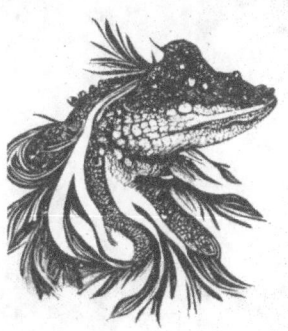

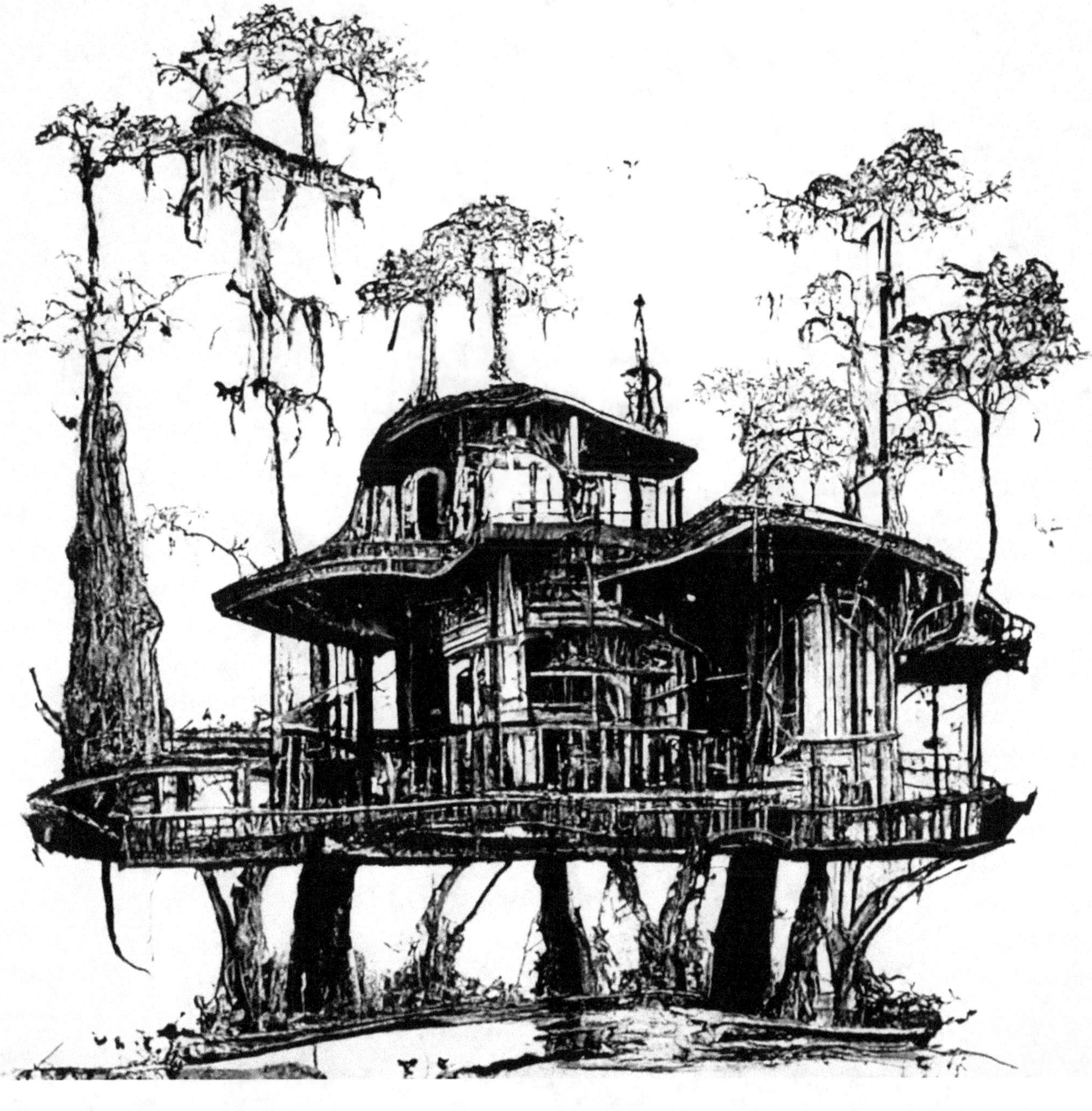

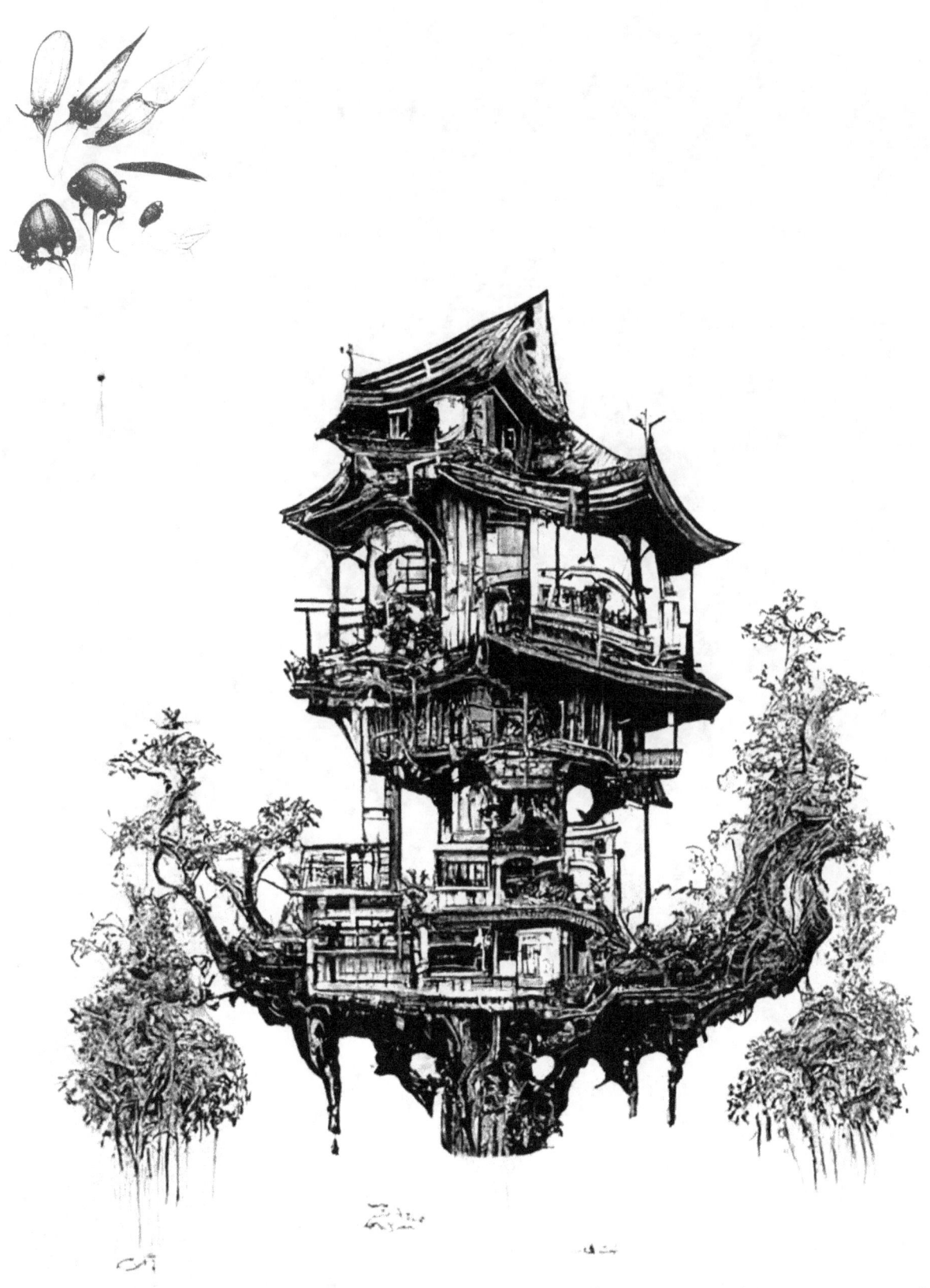

I do love the swamp houses. How practical! No need to worry about rotting piers, instead living wood holds up these homes high over the waters, and as the marginalia indicate, other toothy creatures.

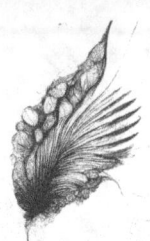

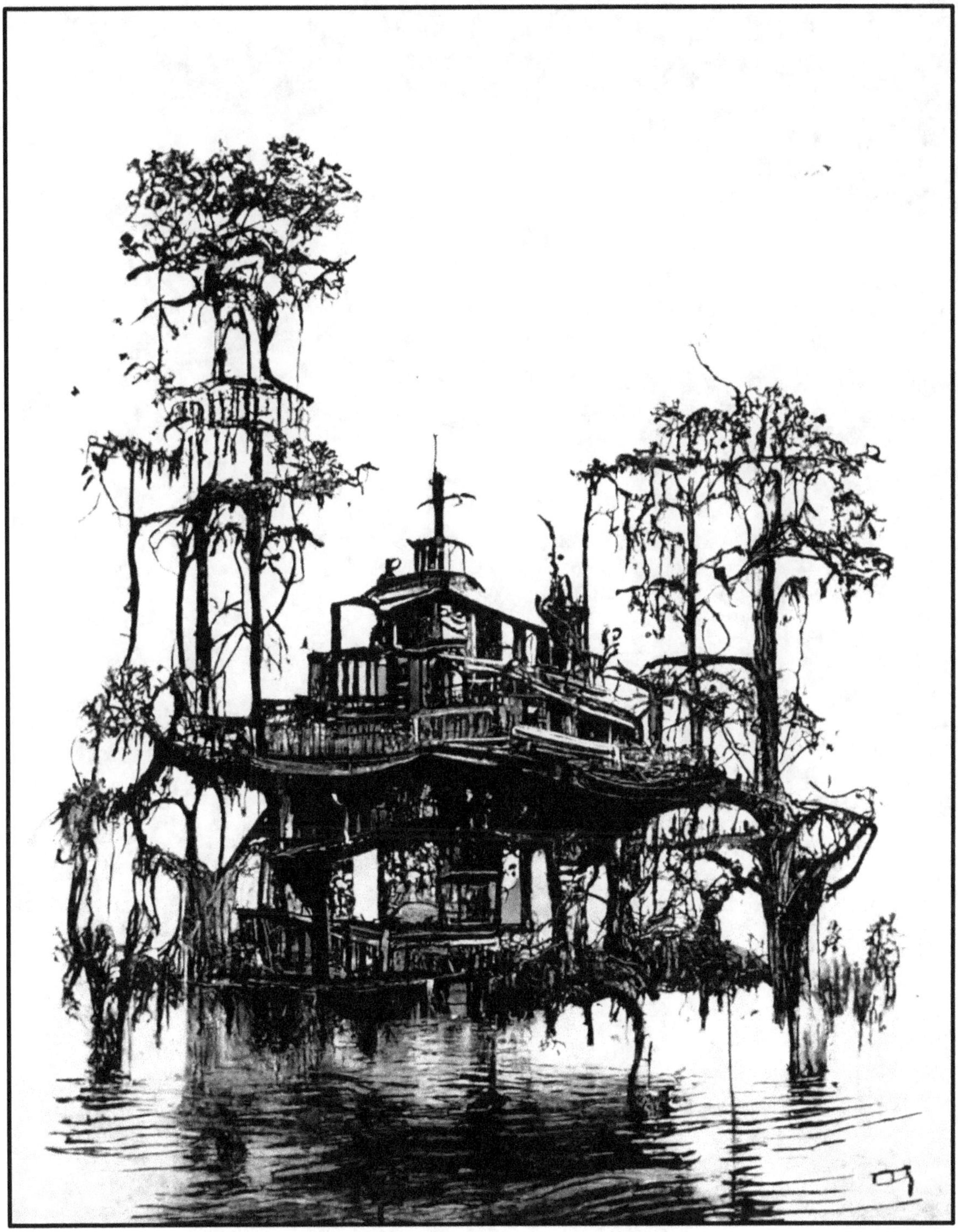

The image speaks to me of moss, and mosquitoes. I'm sure it's a lovely home. To visit.

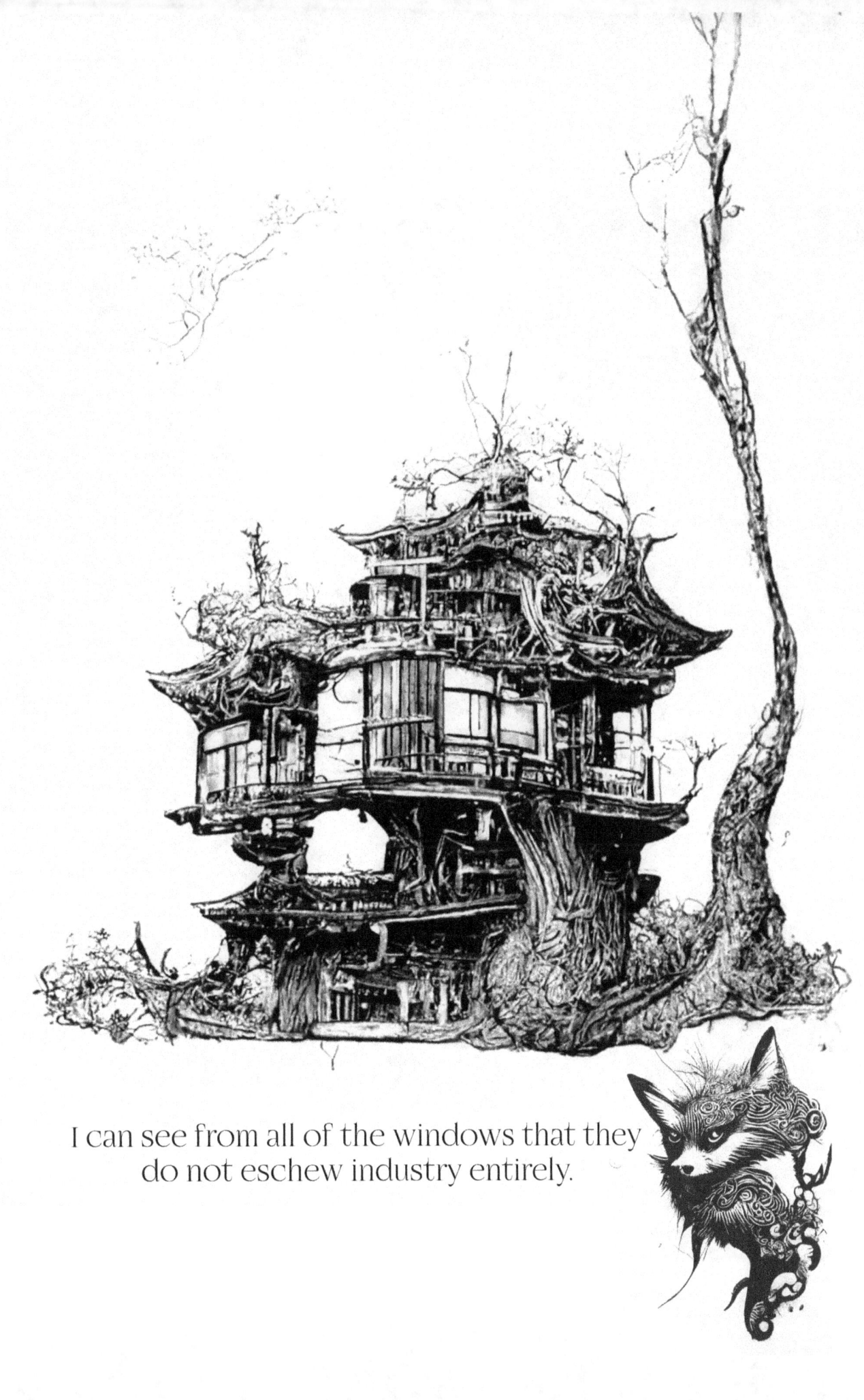

I can see from all of the windows that they do not eschew industry entirely.

Lashed to enormous branches, this home sprawls out far more than most of them do. 𝒨𝓂𝑒 𝒦's inclusion here of a cat in ornate garb intrigues me. I have so many questions about the proportions of the inhabitants!

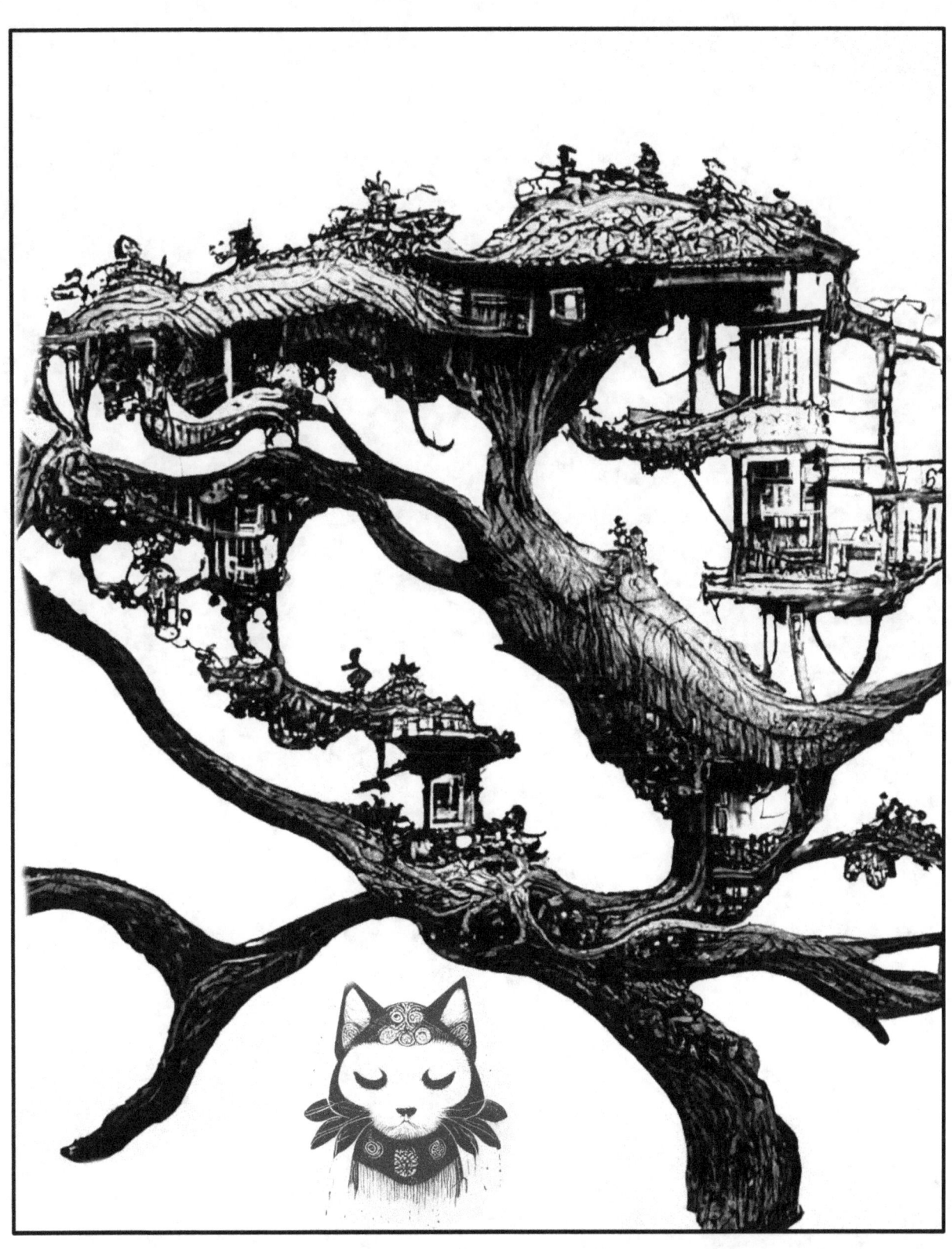

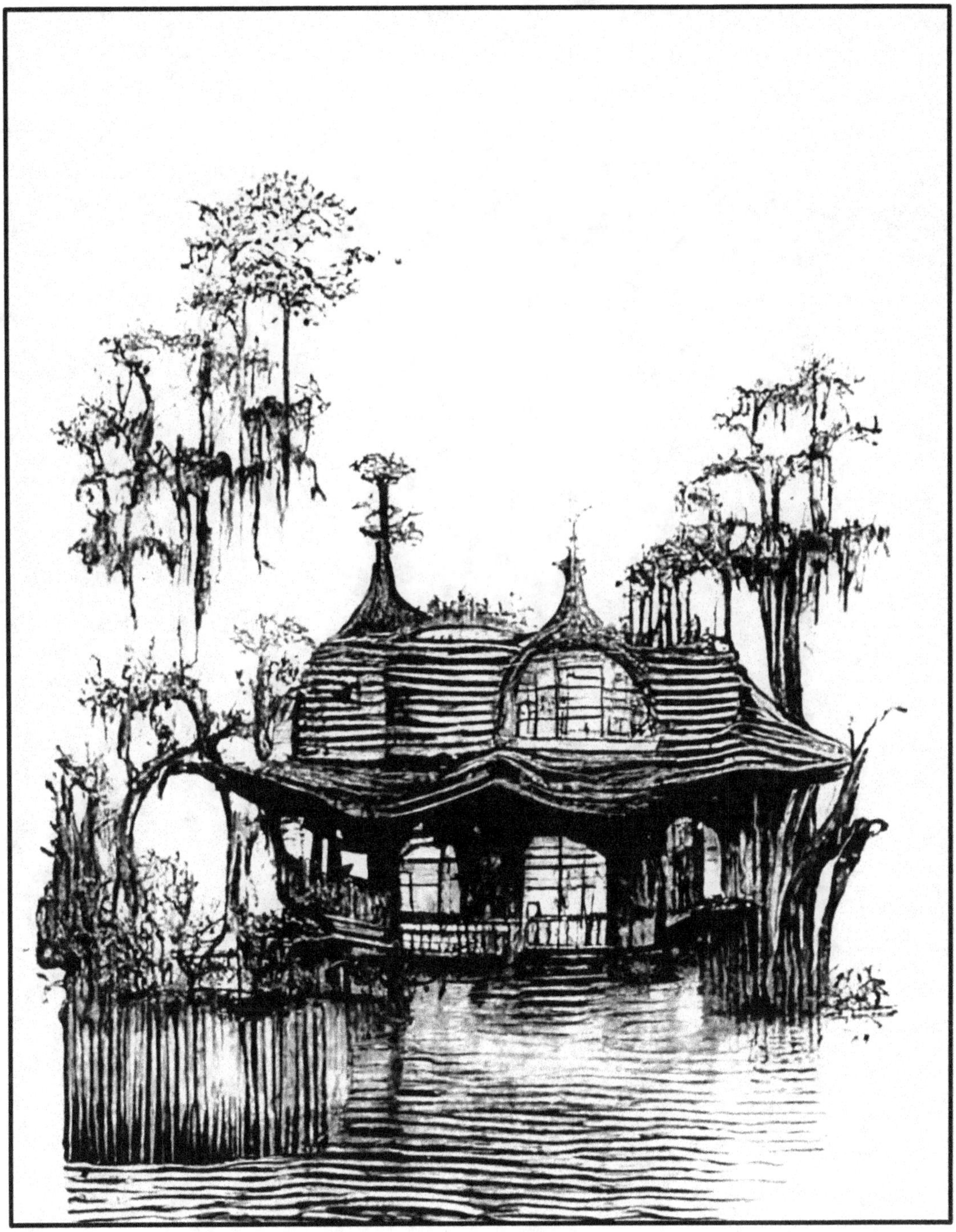

Deep in the swamps, where the chickens roost high... This house looks almost like a houseboat, with the water lapping right up to the steps. The trees growing from the roof must root somewhere, though?

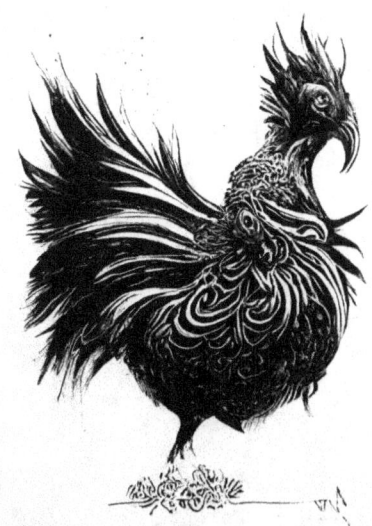

Elsewhere I saw ornithopters in her marginalia, but here we also see a submarine vehicle in conjunction with a swamp home. Hm. Perhaps subtelma? With the Greek for swamp being Telma. I should think navigation would be very difficult with the muds and currents here!

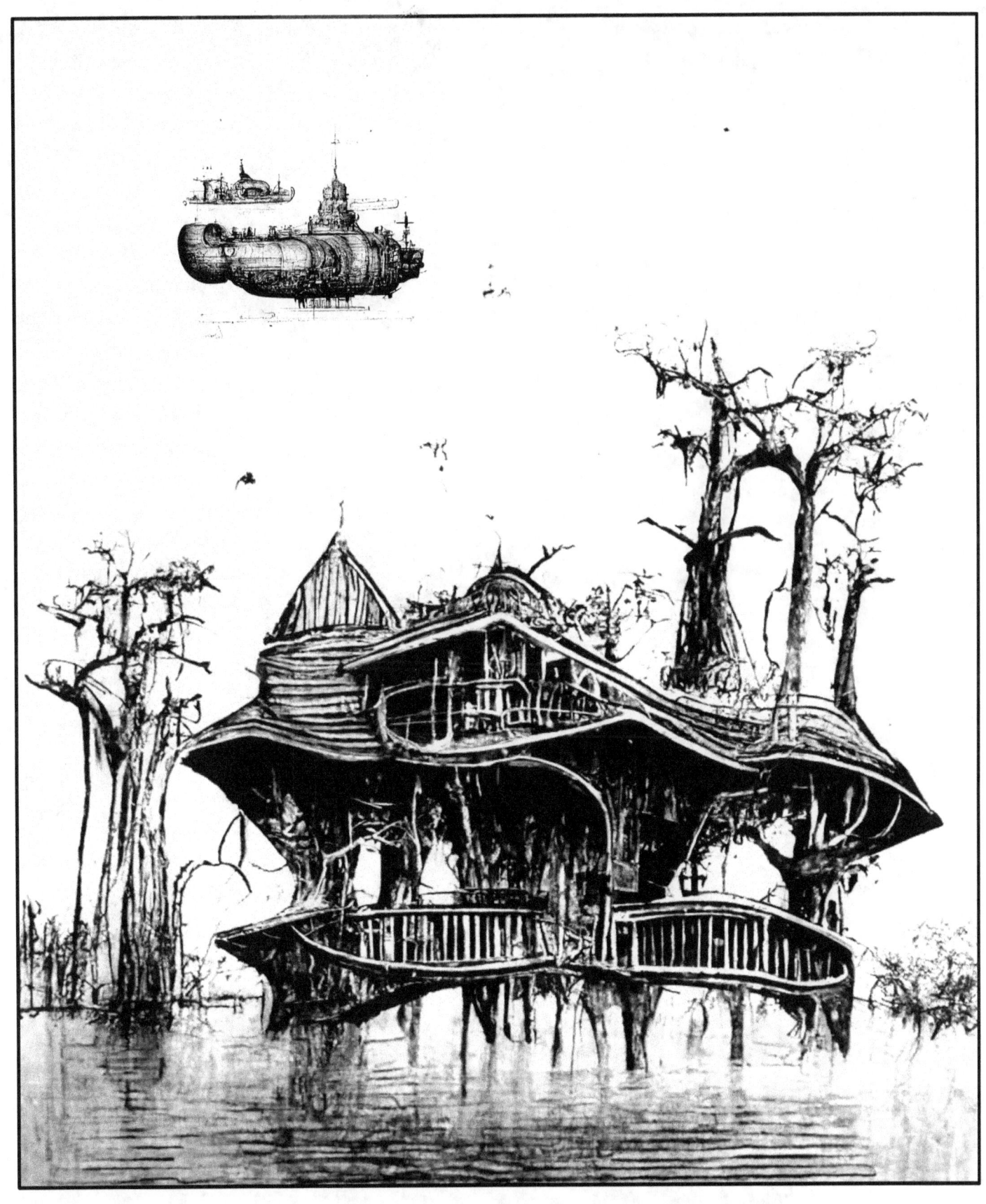

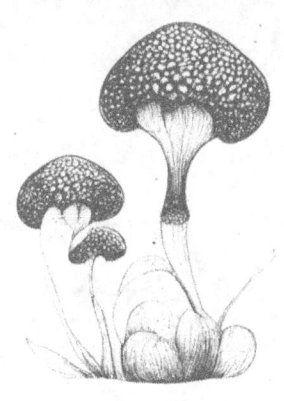

This house looks worse for wear. I do wonder what they do with old houses. Demolition? Or simply let the mushrooms take the wood back to forest humus and begin anew?

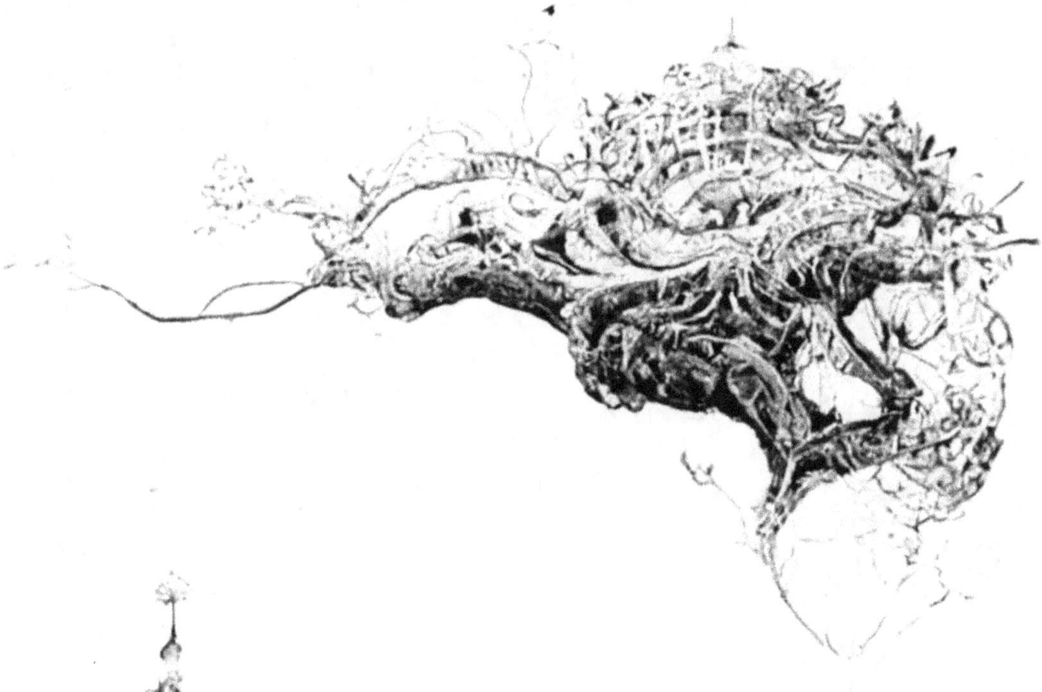

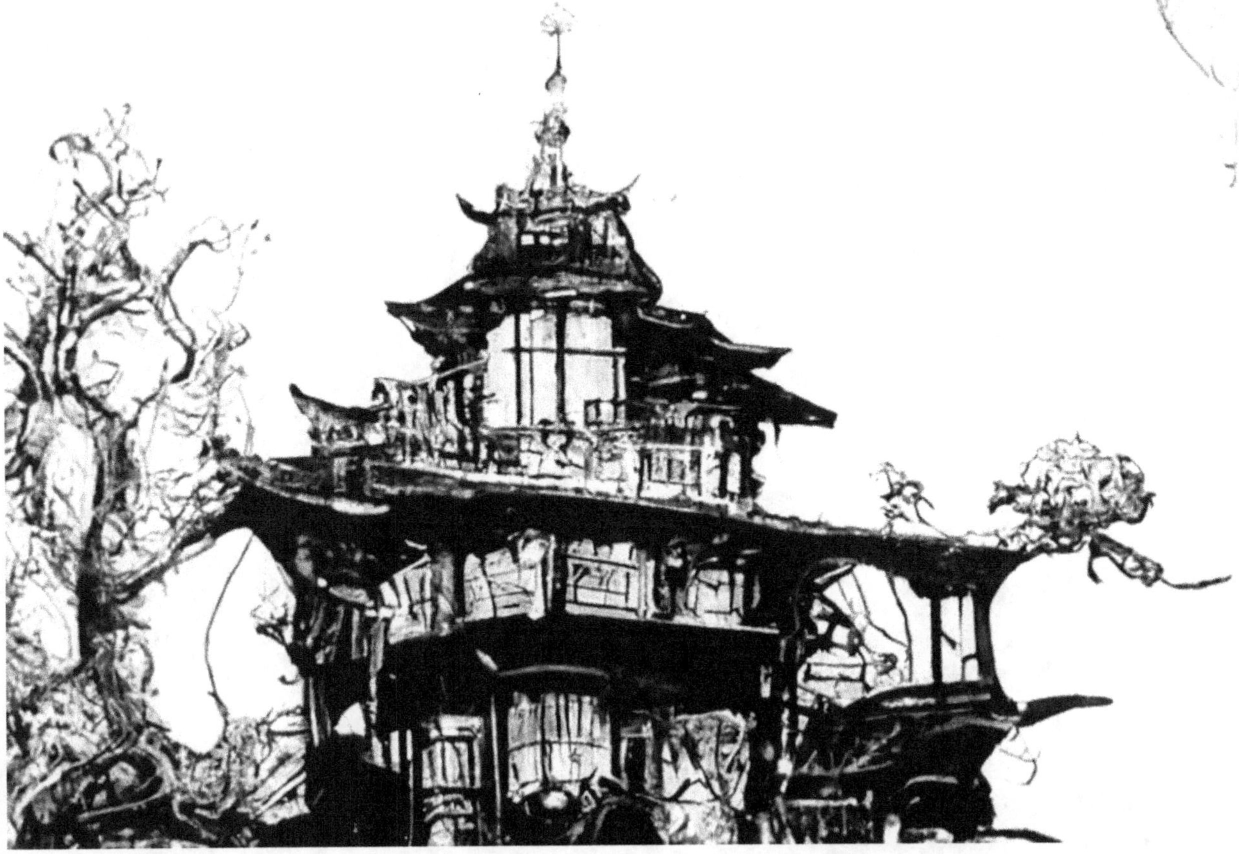

Another subtelma boat! Maybe I should go with a Latin root, to match the prefix. Subpalus? At any rate, this home seems to have a passage to semi-solid land by wrapping around a secondary tree with conveniently sloped trunk.

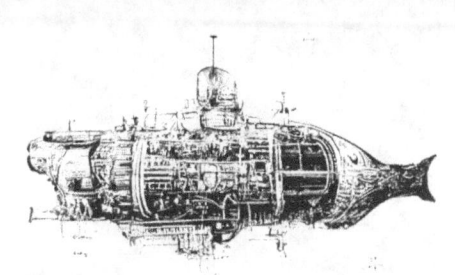

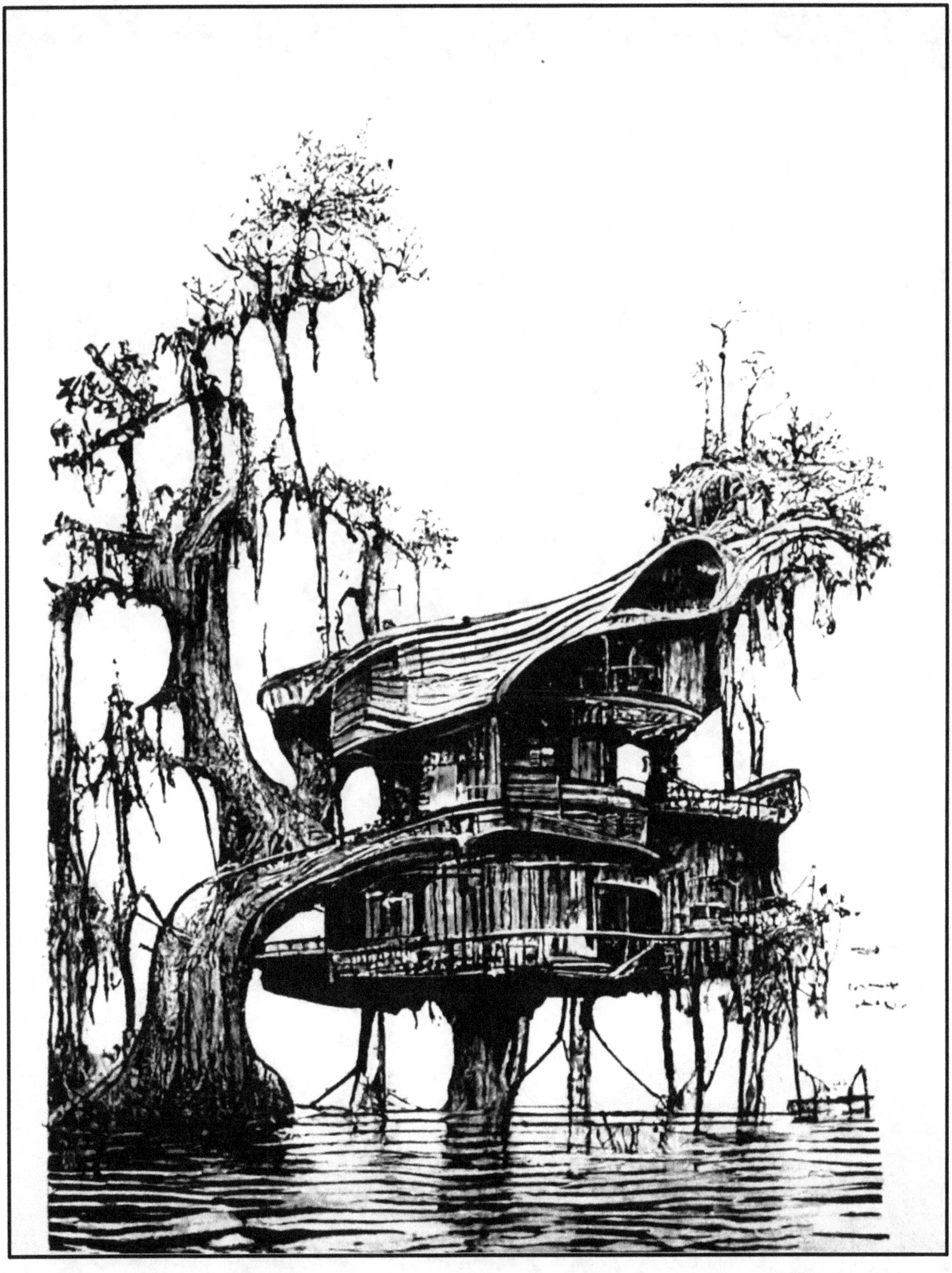

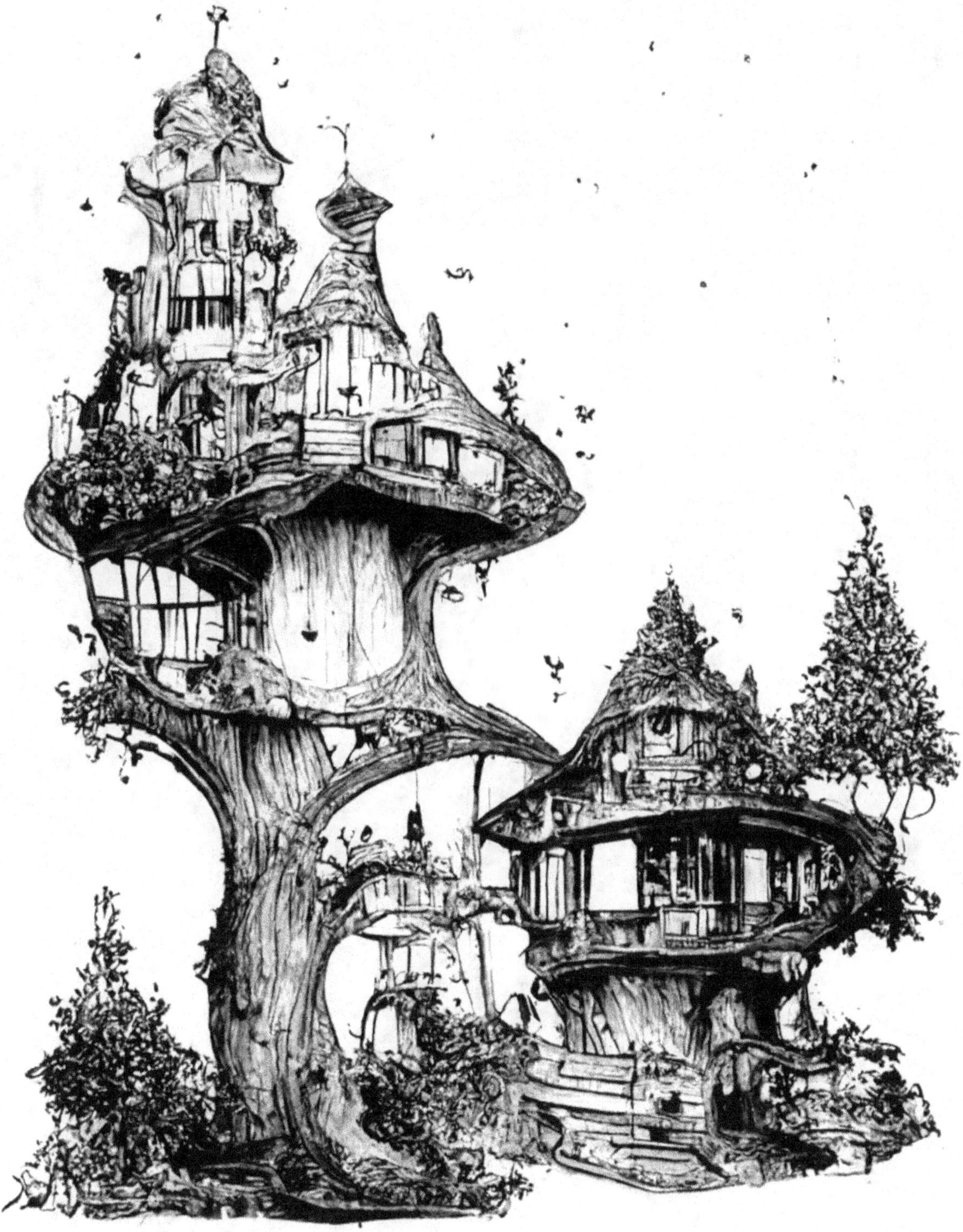

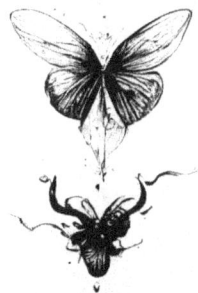

Some of the home are more stumphouses than treehouses. Much less romantic a term, that. Still, these can't possibly be living trees used as the central supports. Not enough foliage to sustain them.

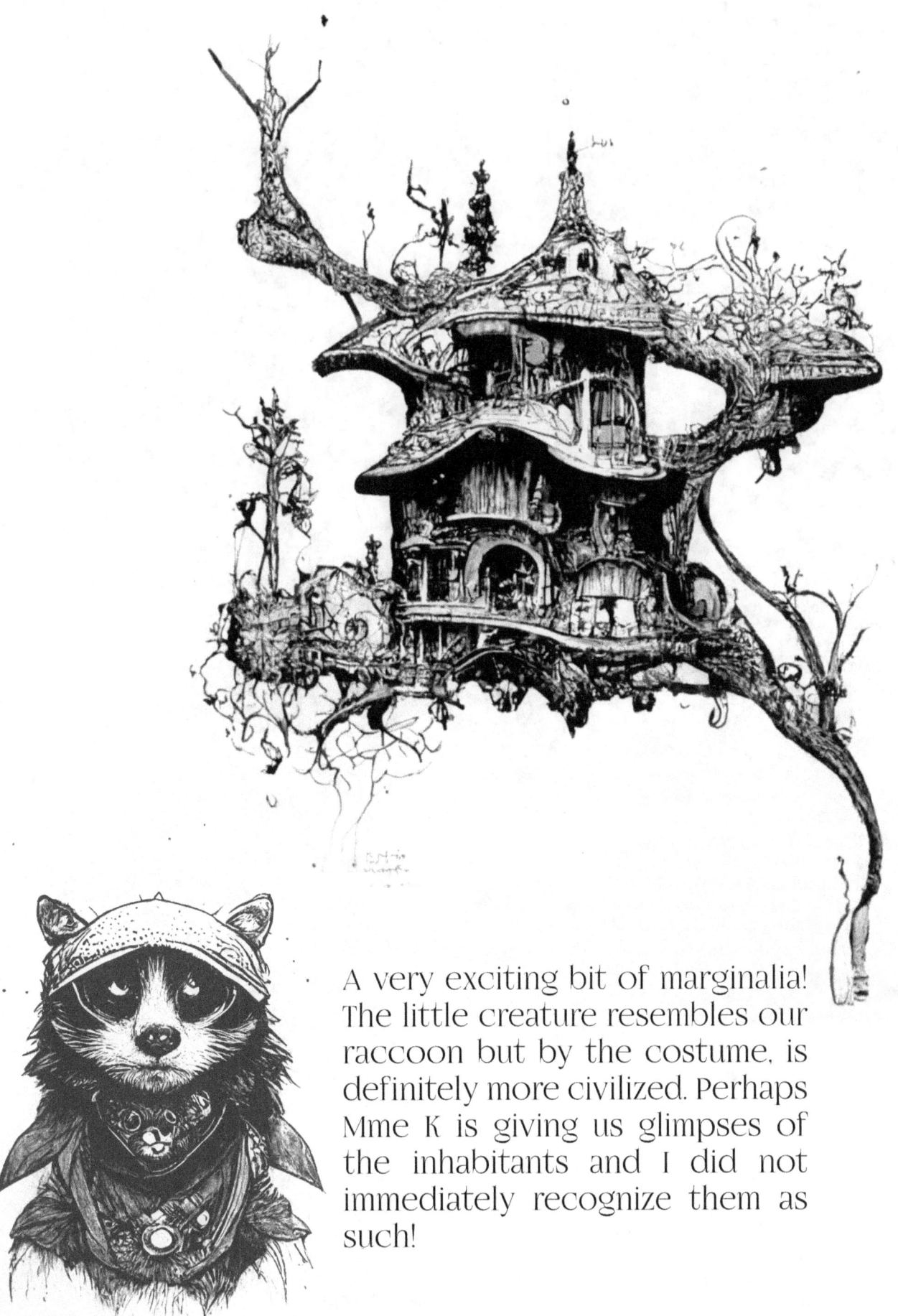

A very exciting bit of marginalia! The little creature resembles our raccoon but by the costume, is definitely more civilized. Perhaps Mme K is giving us glimpses of the inhabitants and I did not immediately recognize them as such!

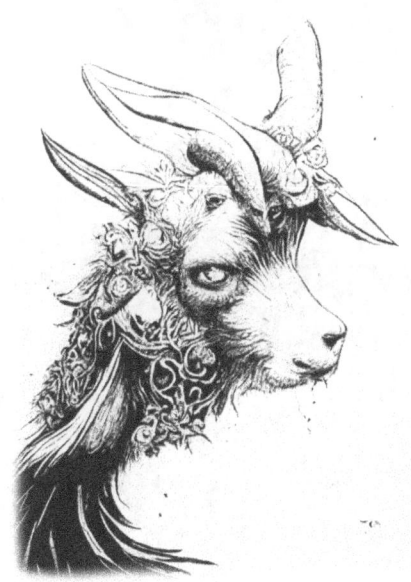

Again, the jaunty hat on this goat leads me to believe that I am seeing a faery creature, not a poor dumb beast of our own world. A charming domicile for such, if he boasts two feet and has thumbs!

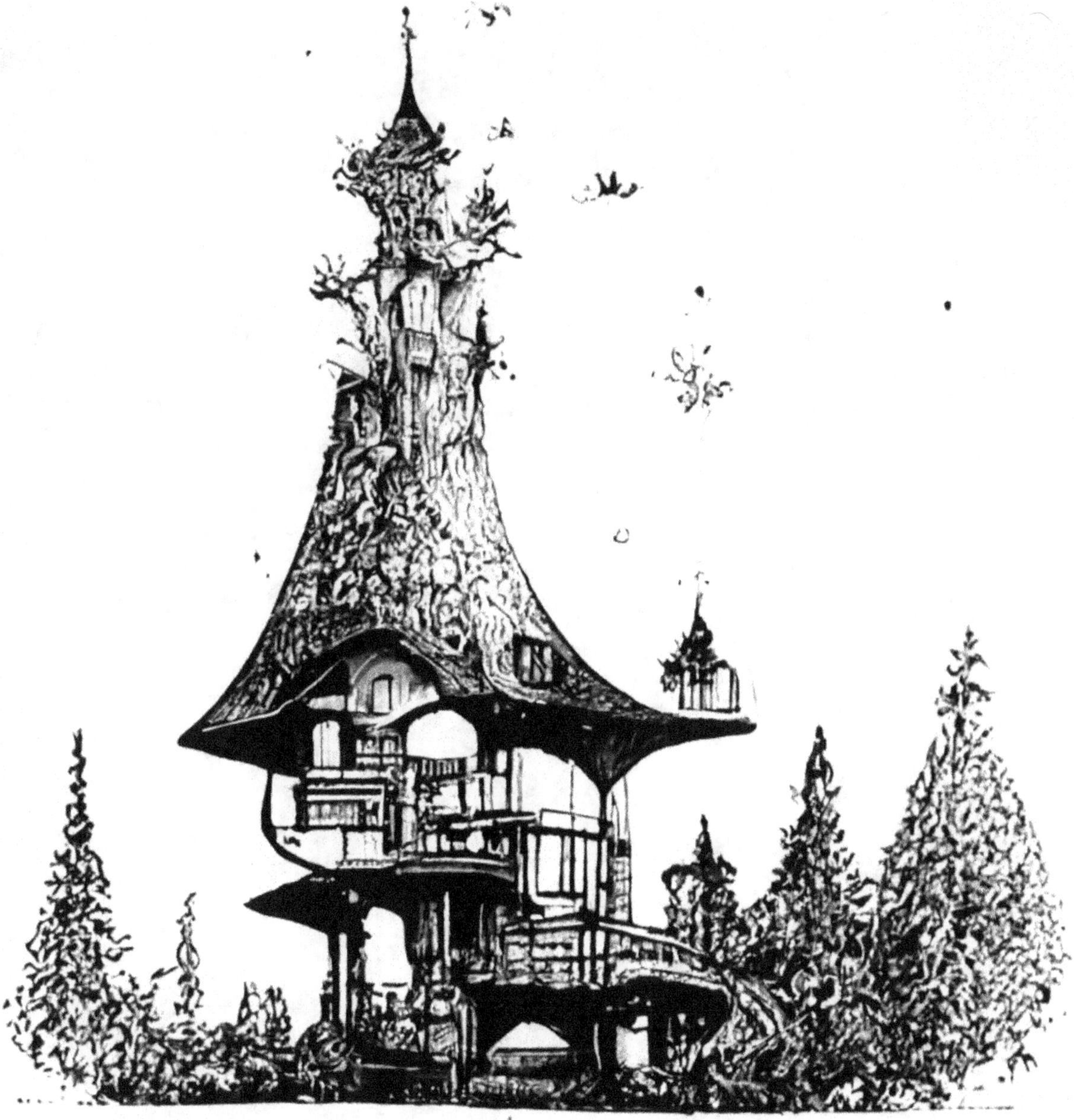

I do love the little porch off on the branch. There must be an easy way to reach it, though. From this drawing it appears one would have to go down and over, not something I'd care to attempt prior to my morning coffee!

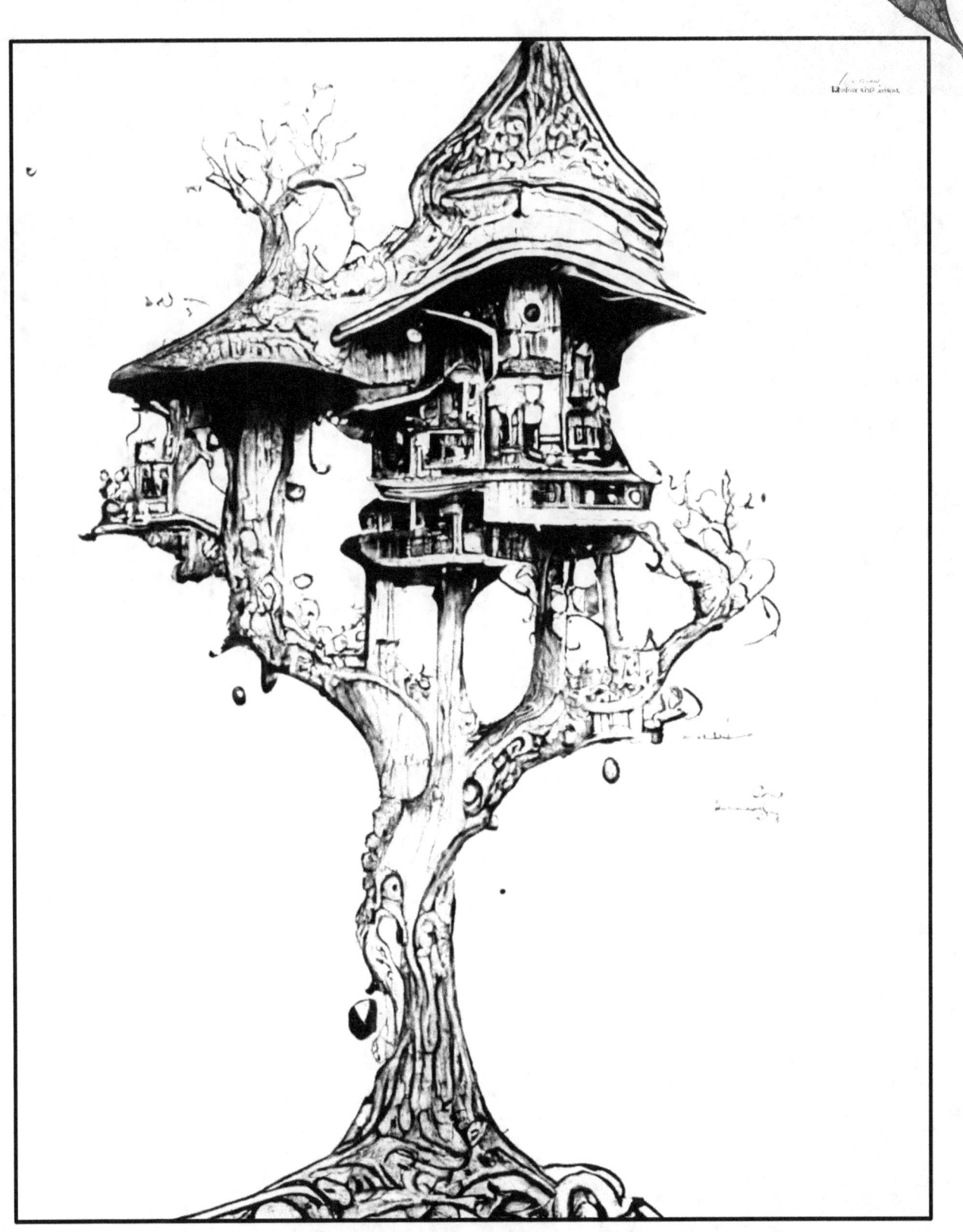

The perspective here is odd. Is this suspended? Is there a trunk out of sight? Are branches grafted decades prior to construction? How far ahead do their architects plan?

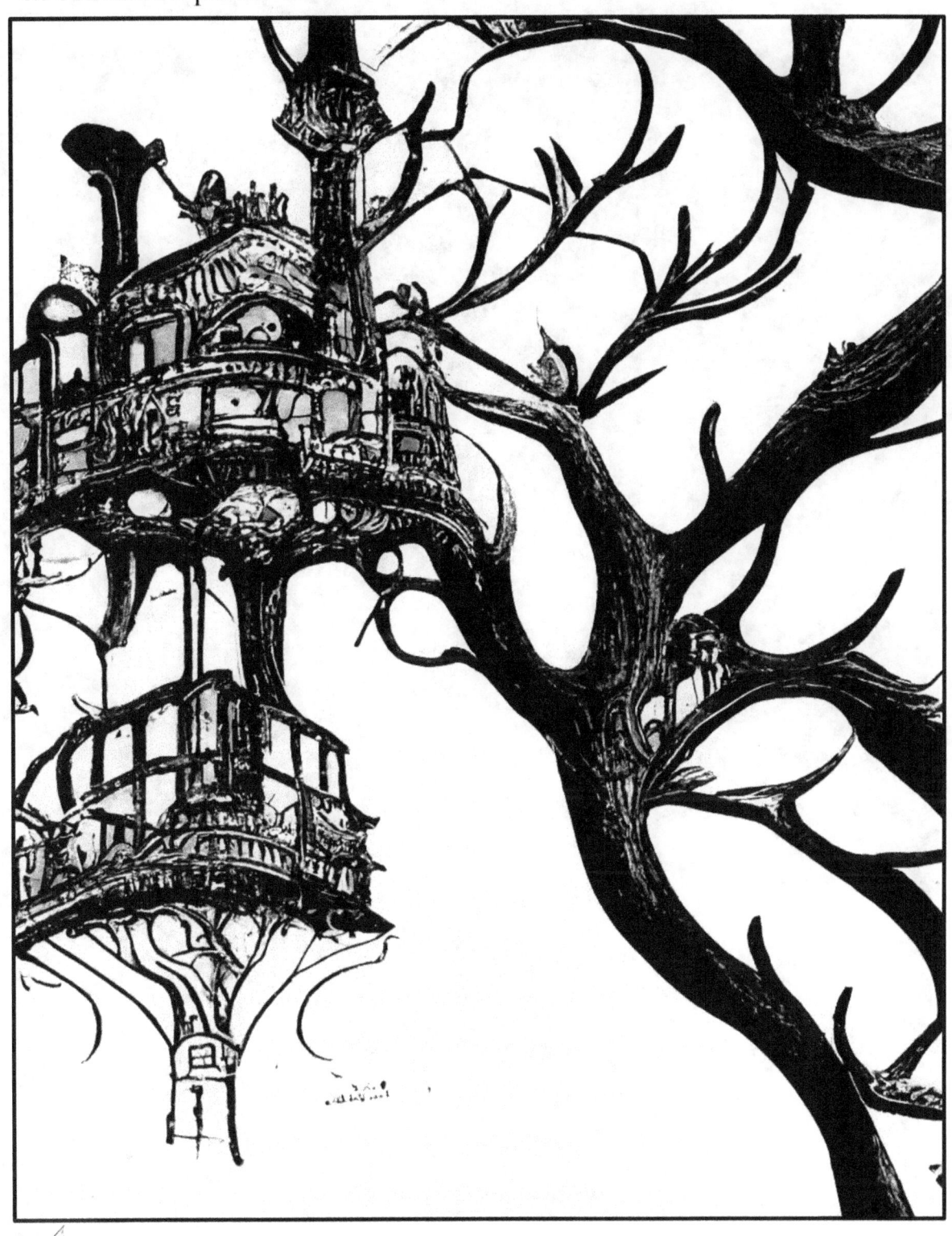

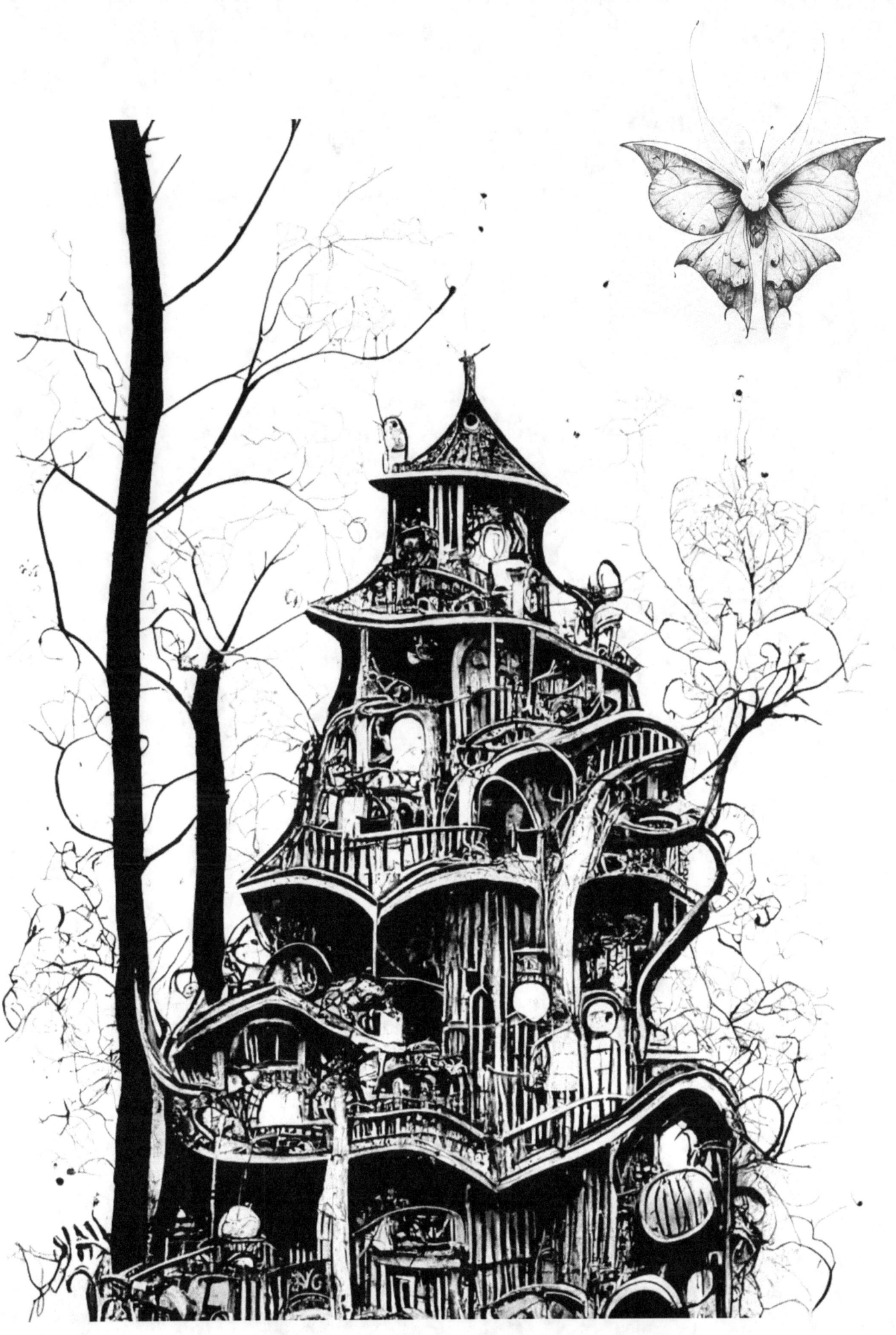

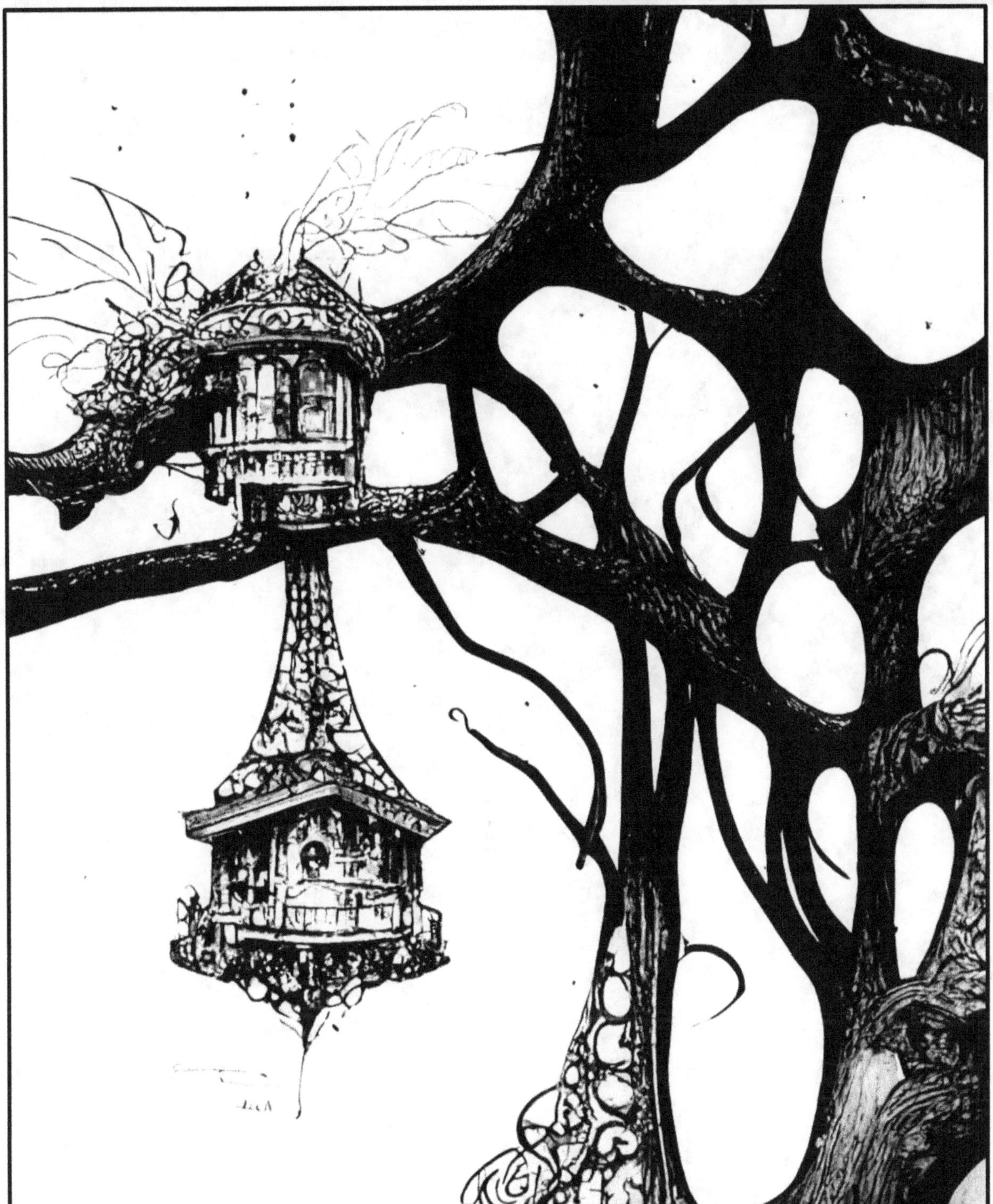

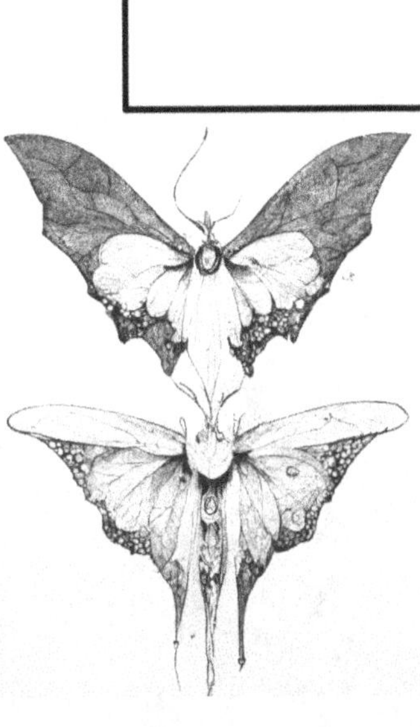

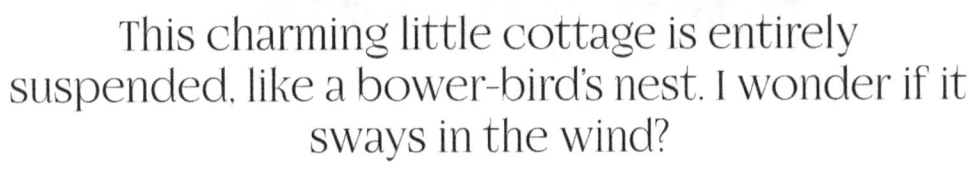

This charming little cottage is entirely suspended, like a bower-bird's nest. I wonder if it sways in the wind?

She has not included color much in her drawings, apologizing for lack of pure pigments that could survive, using a word I cannot translate. Here, though, I think there is stained glass of remarkably vivid coloring.

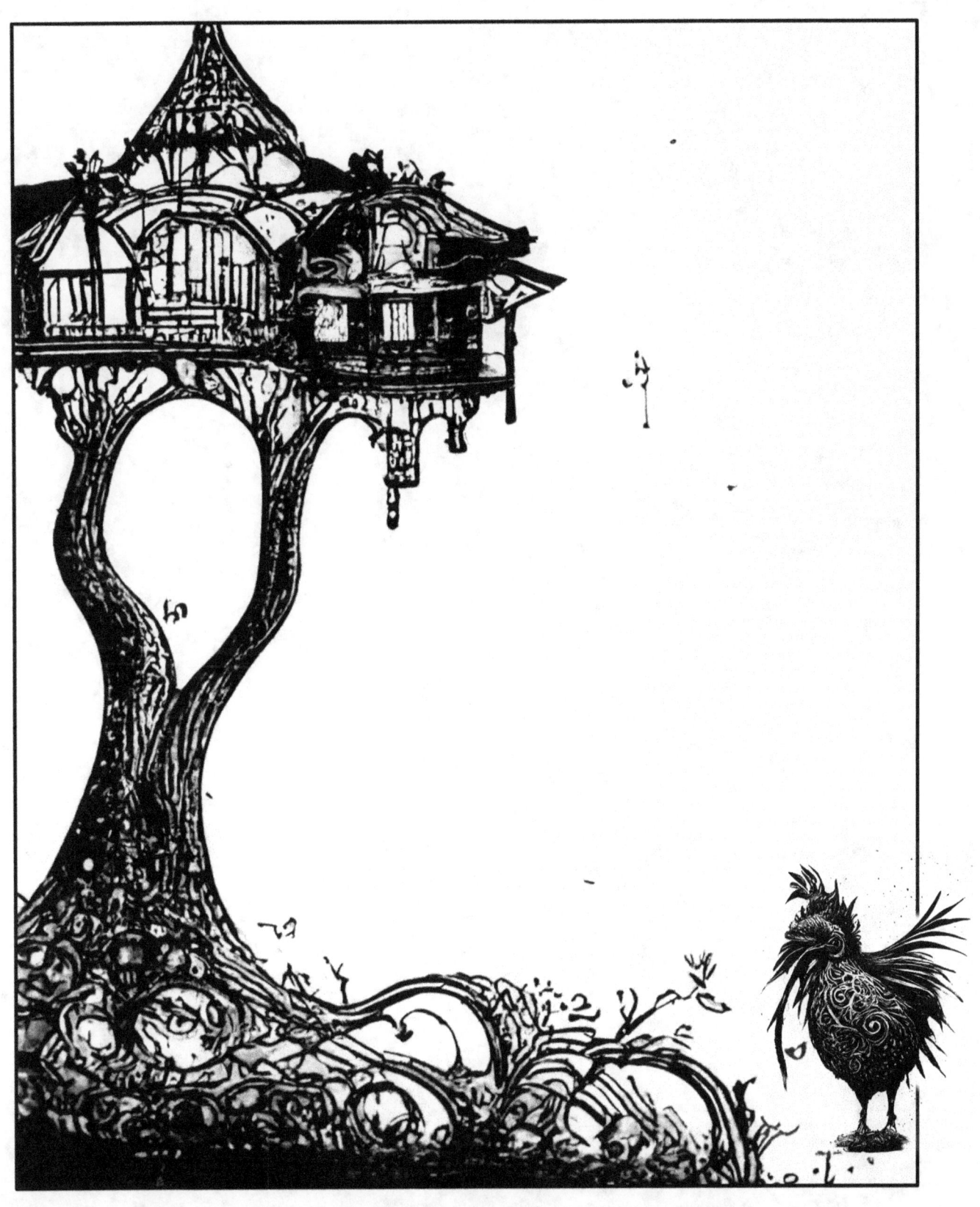

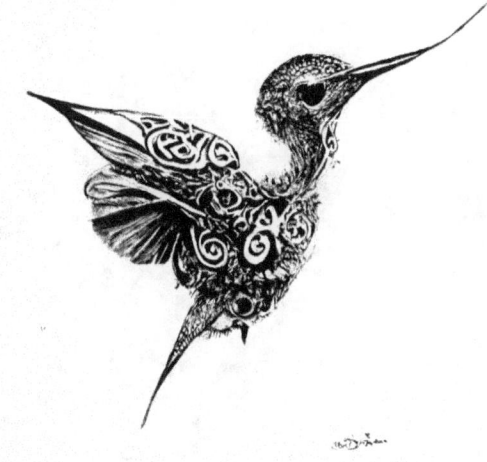

Mme K notes this house as being a 'representative dwelling of the *staerlings*.' I am uncertain if she perhaps means the bird-simulacra, although perhaps not as she notes under it that it is an *mcDyrbin*.

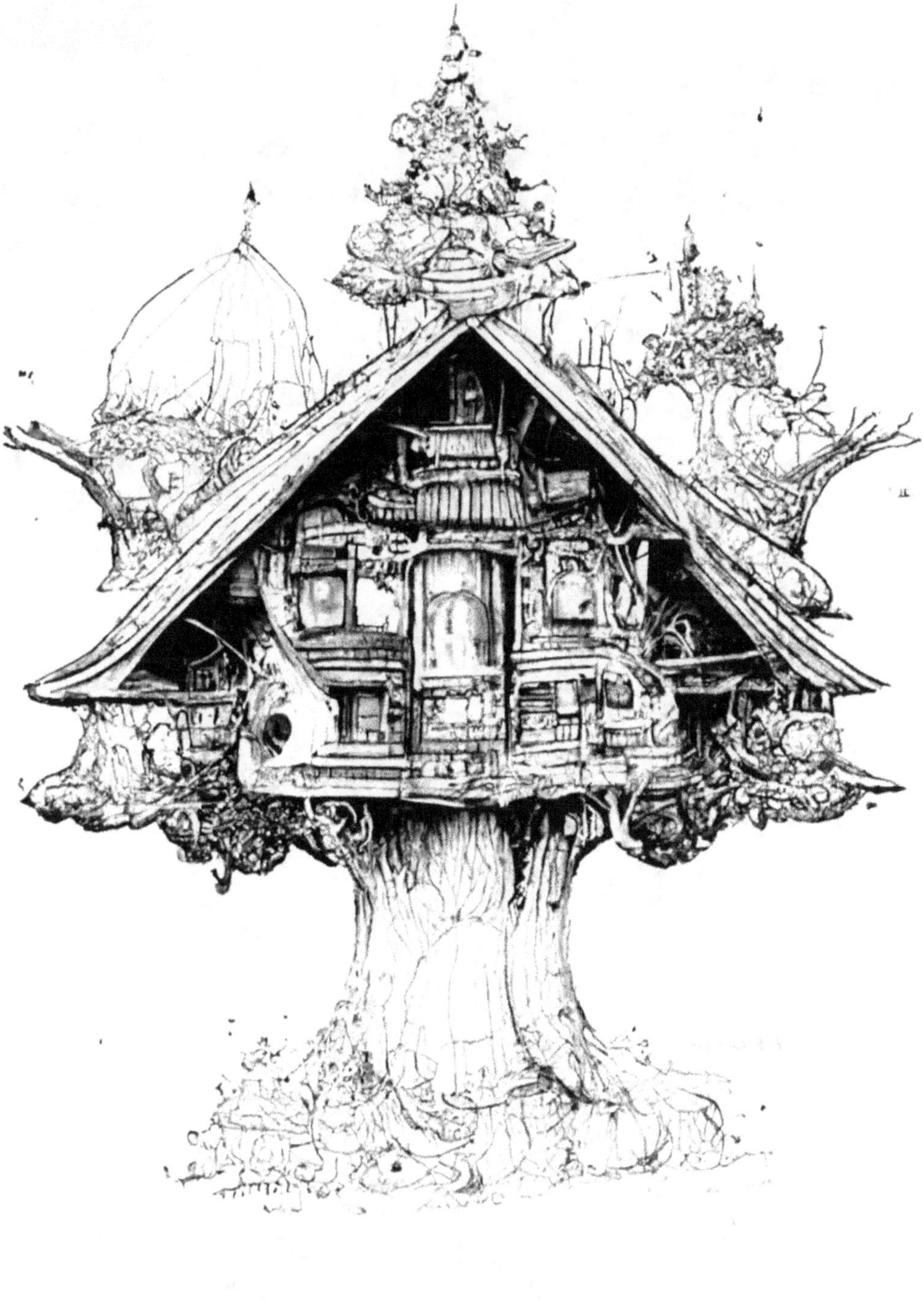

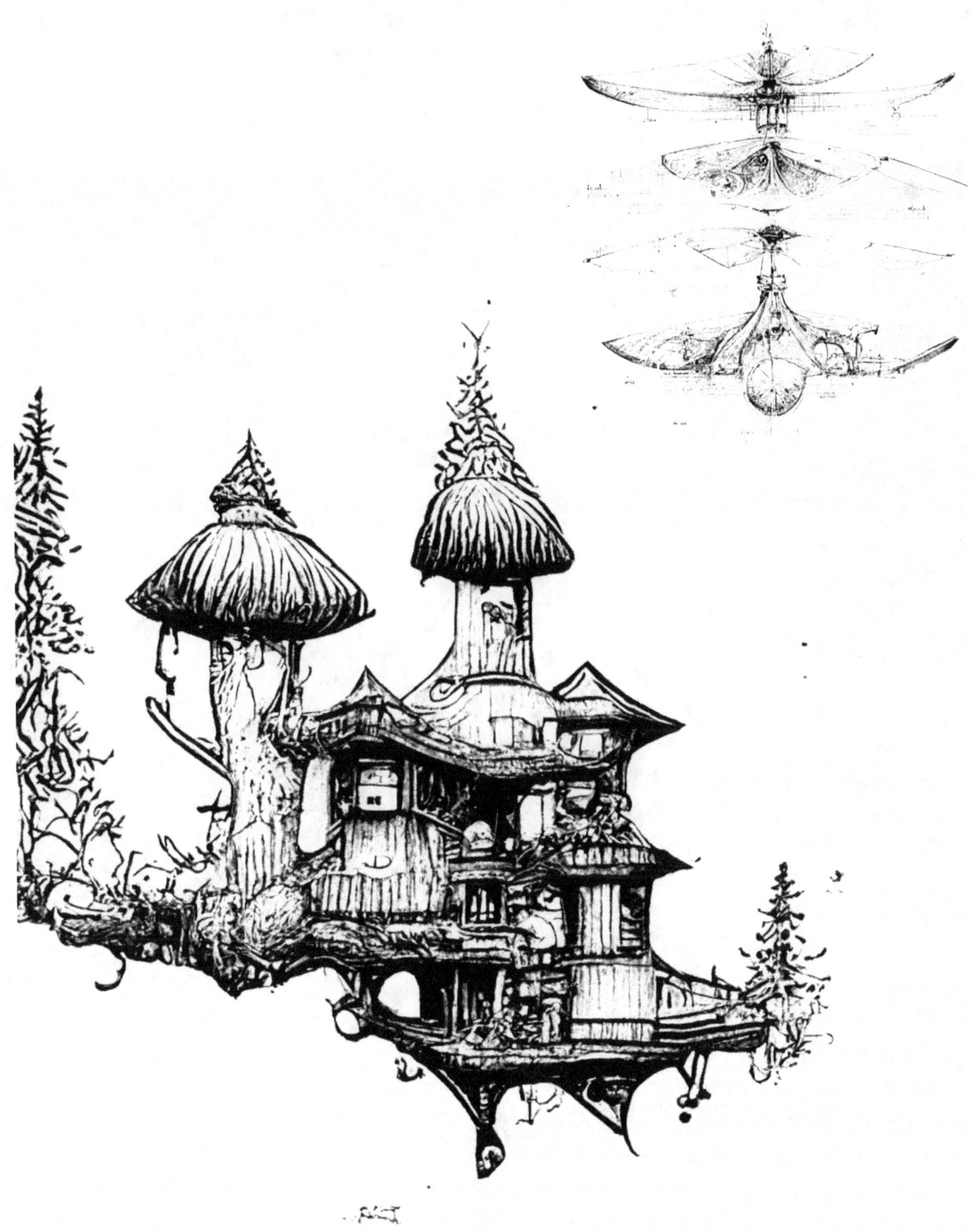

Thatched roofs make this cottage compound look a little like mushrooms. The ornithopters made a reappearance in her marginalia, with such tiny notes I cannot possibly make them out.

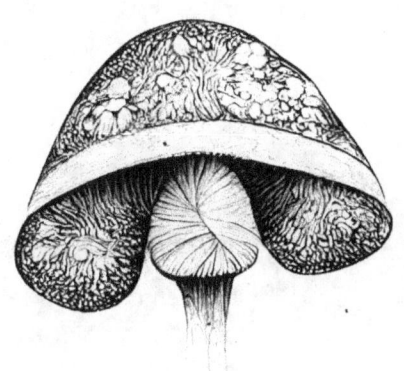

This treehouse has such a pleasant aspect. I can imagine the windows warmly lit by candlelight from within. I've seen no sign of electric wires. Perhaps they have none?

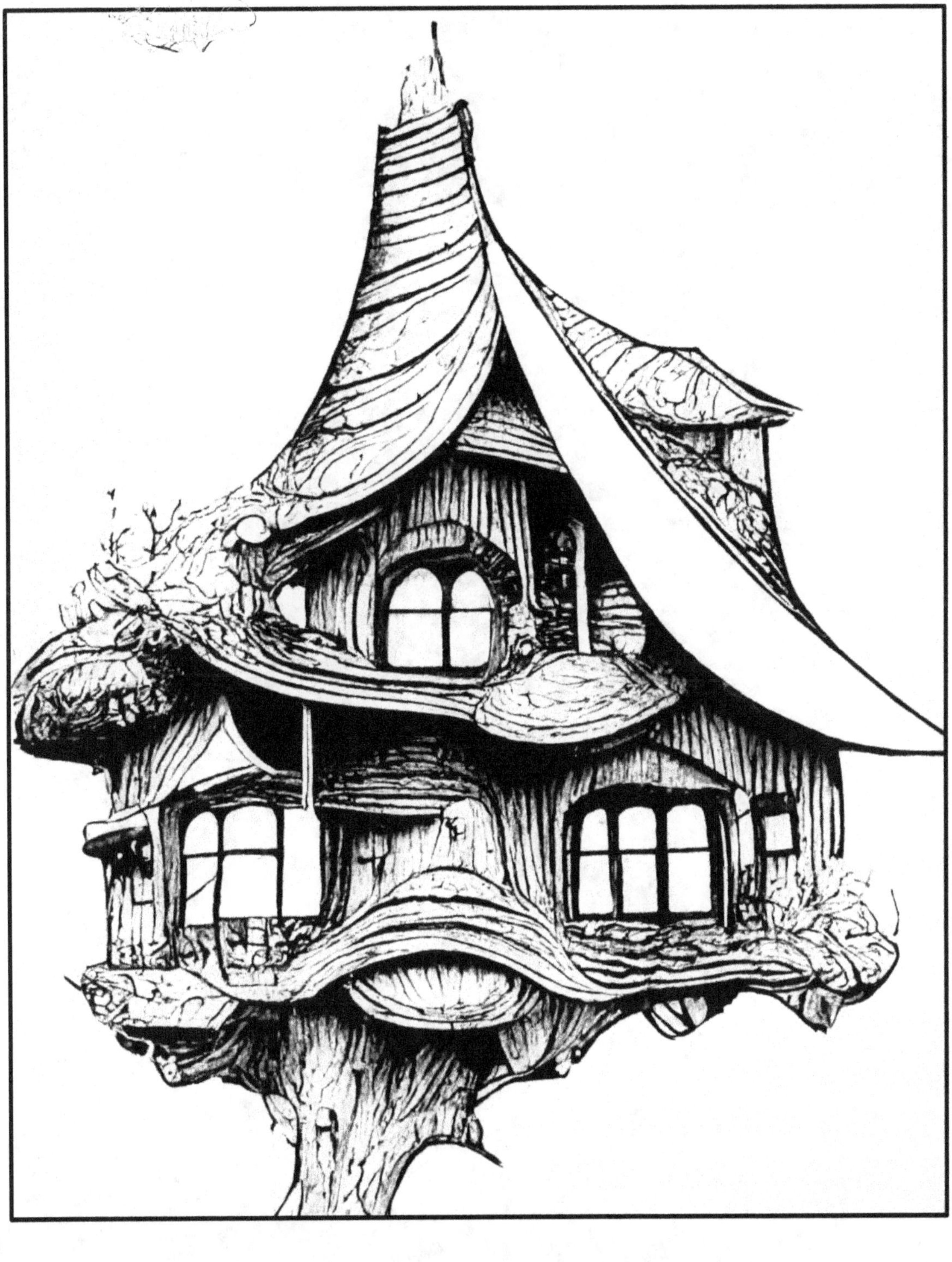

Not only are there no ugly electric lines, nor telephone wires, there seem to be few places recognizable as garages. I suppose the stairs leading to the entrance here may conceal an ornithopter hangar on the other side of the tree, out of sight.

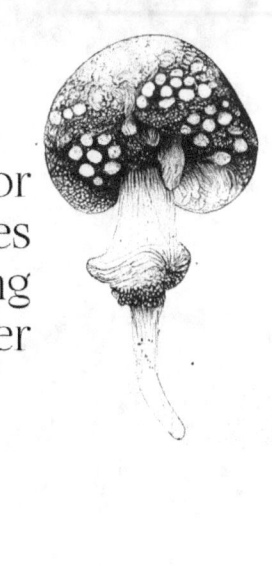

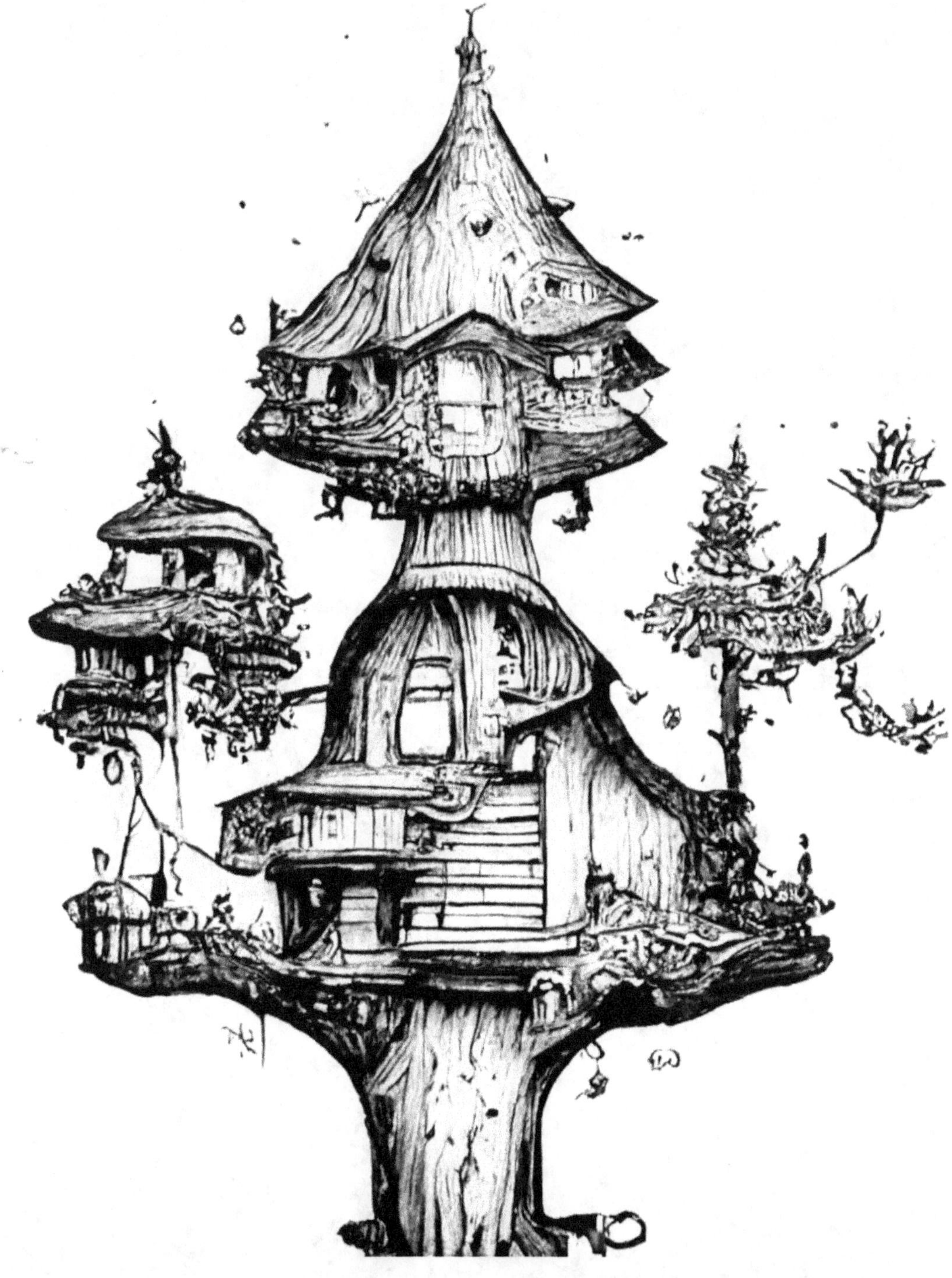

I have dubbed this the Tanuki House, for the marginalia included with it.

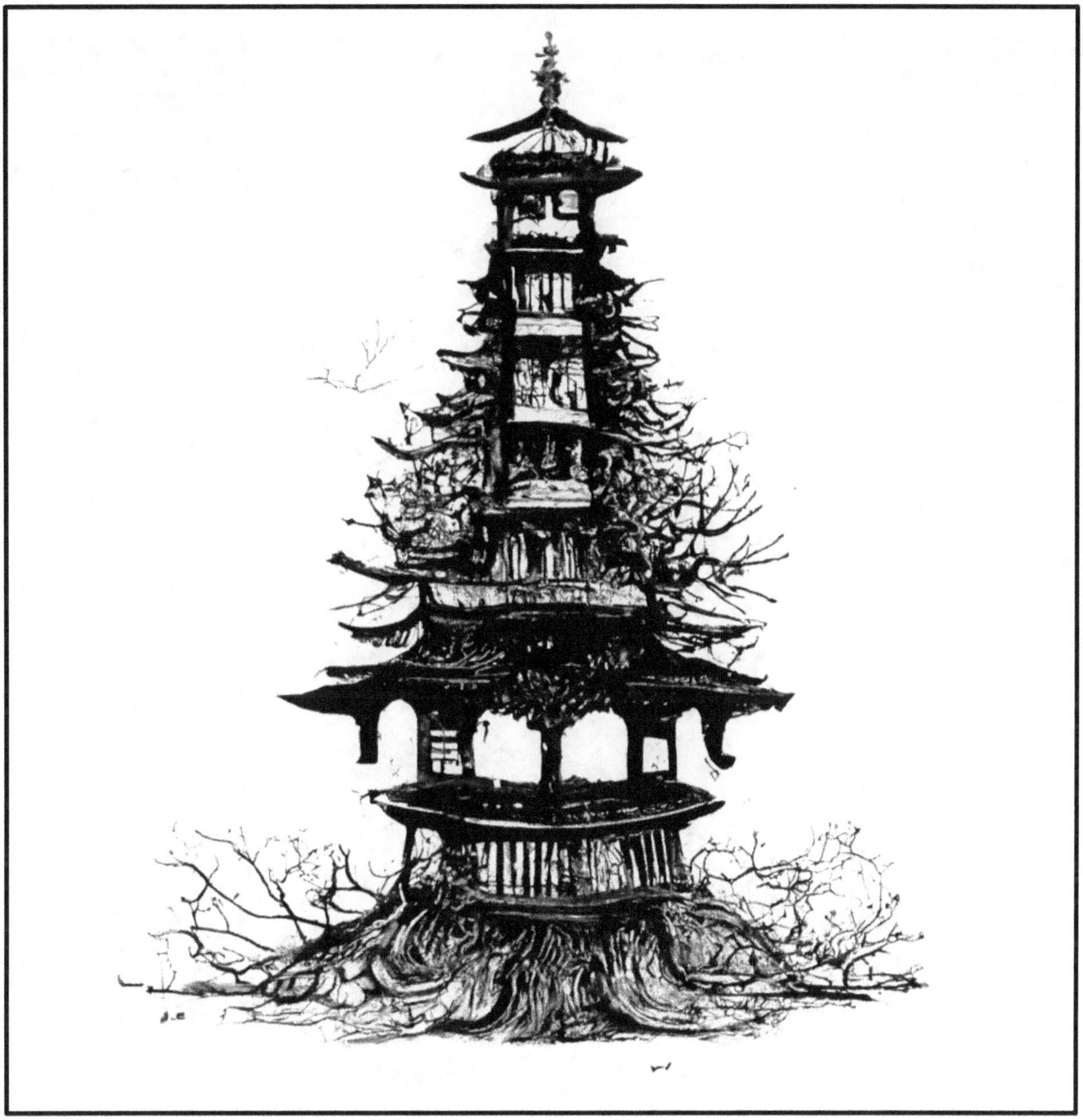

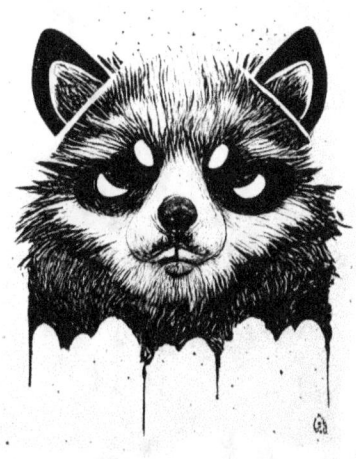

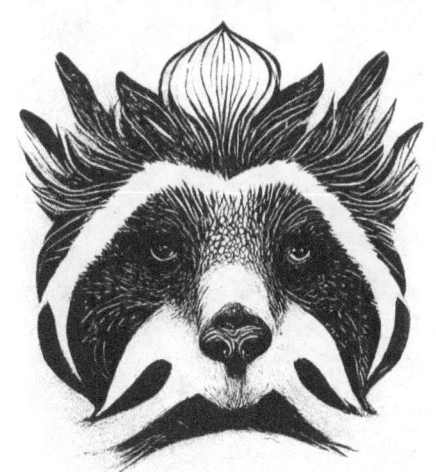

Of all the little creatures, some species strongly resembling our raccoon seems to be prevalent. I can easily see their clever hands building such intricate dwelling-places.

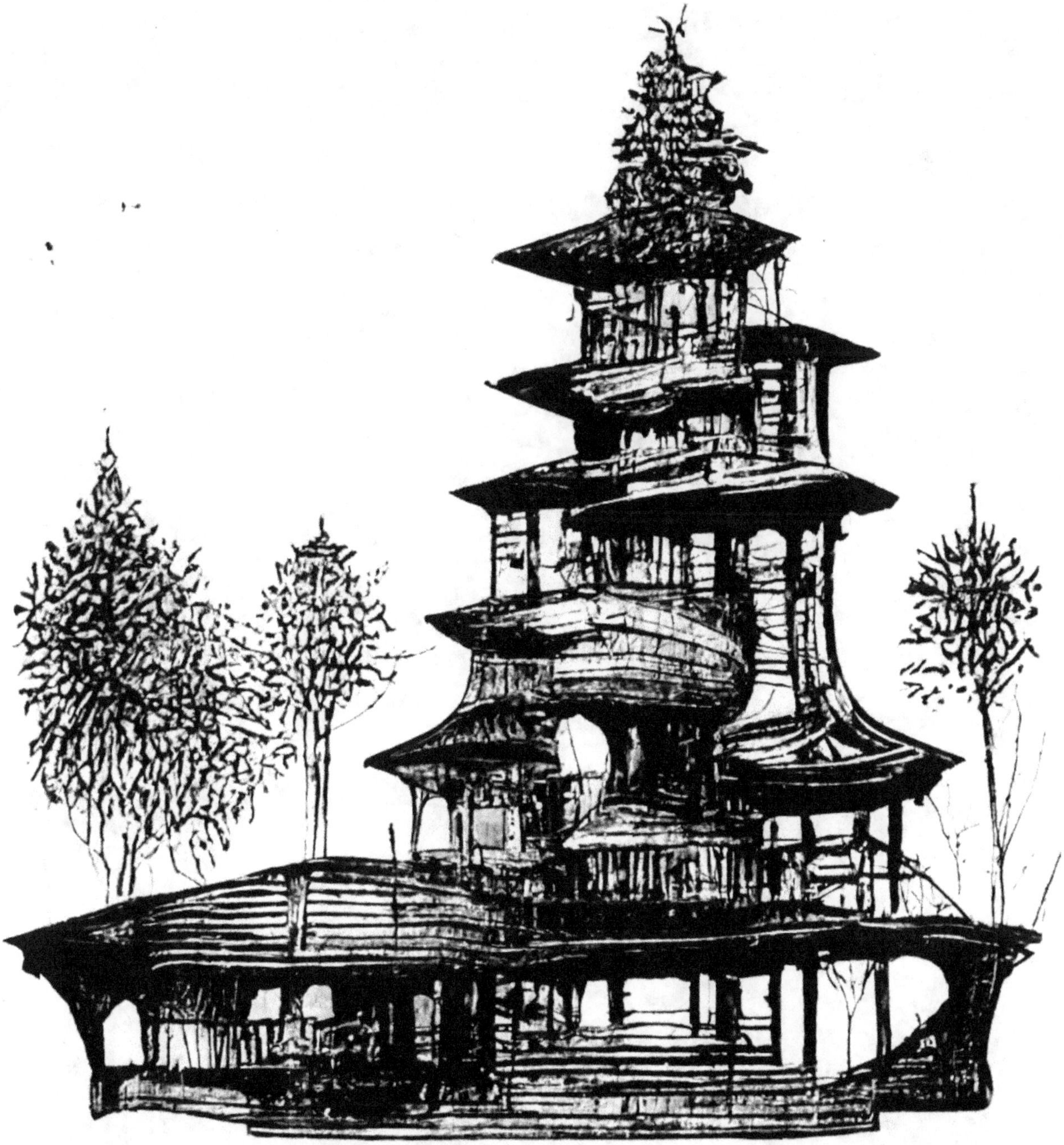

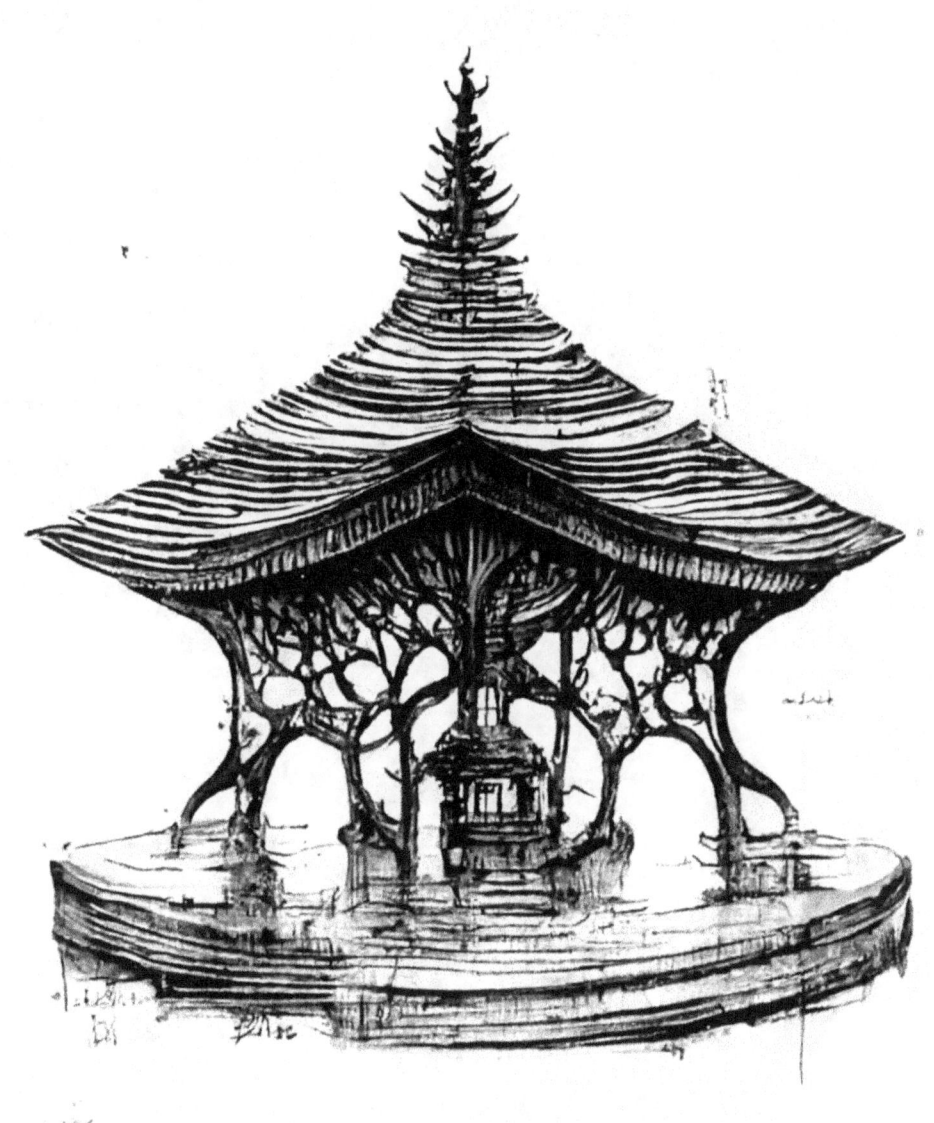

Notes indicate this is a summer kitchen, or perhaps simply a picnic-place, my interpretation is vague at best. The stove in the center implies at least three-season use to my eyes.

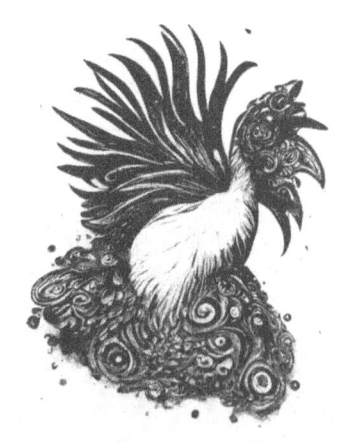

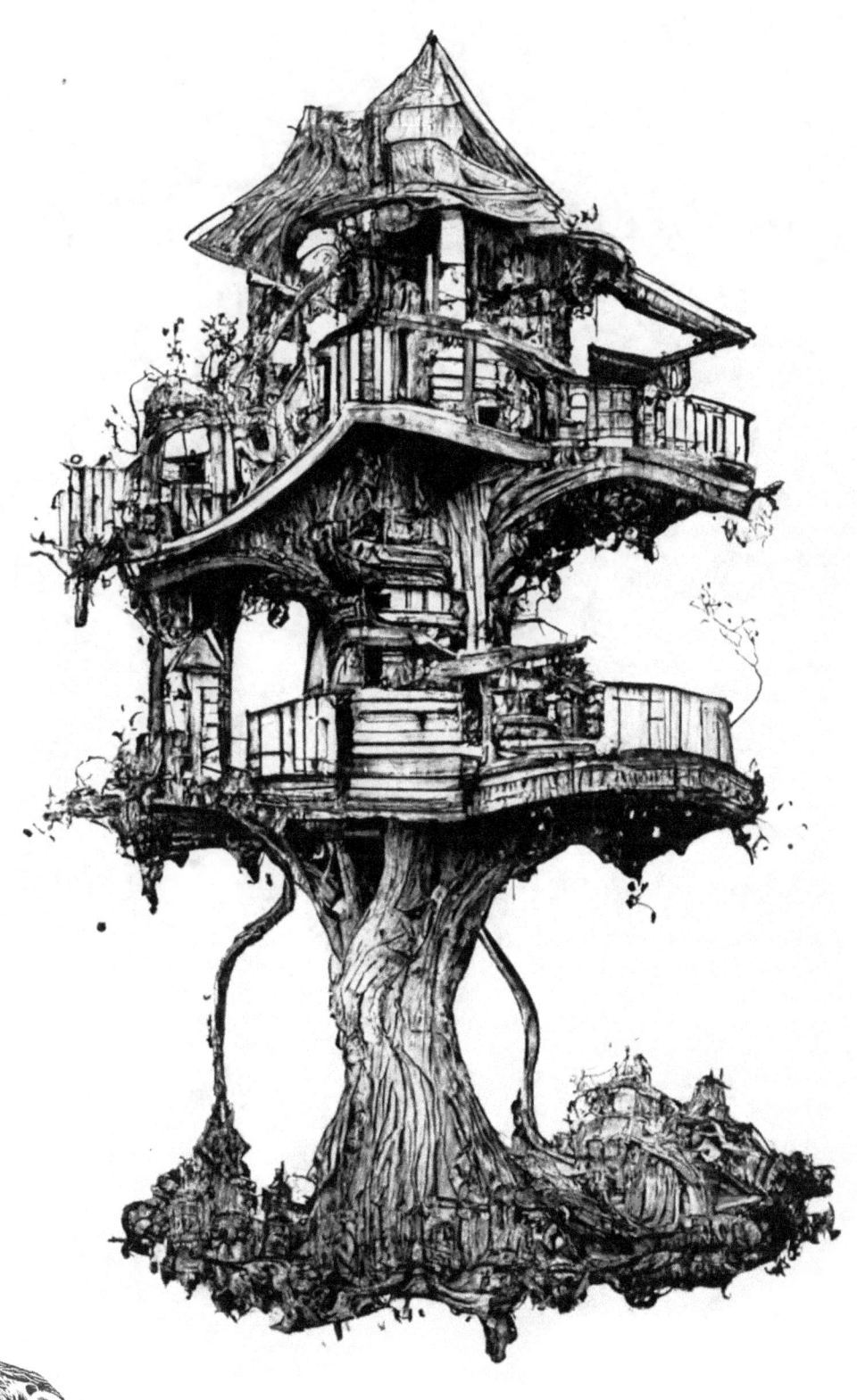

Even the midden-heap under the house is interesting! I can only imagine what you'd find down there, should you dare to dig into it.

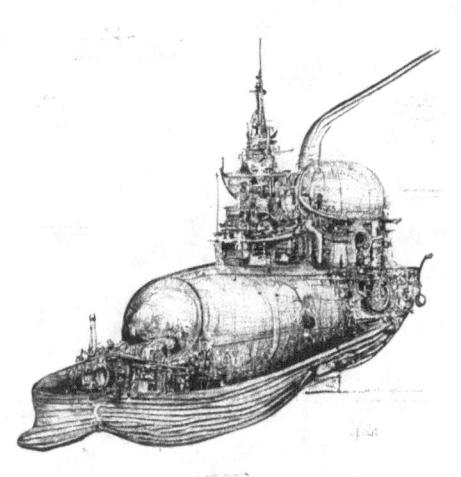

The boat in the marginalia is not intended for submerging, as her notes indicate it's draft, along with notes on what seems to be a complex steam propulsion system.

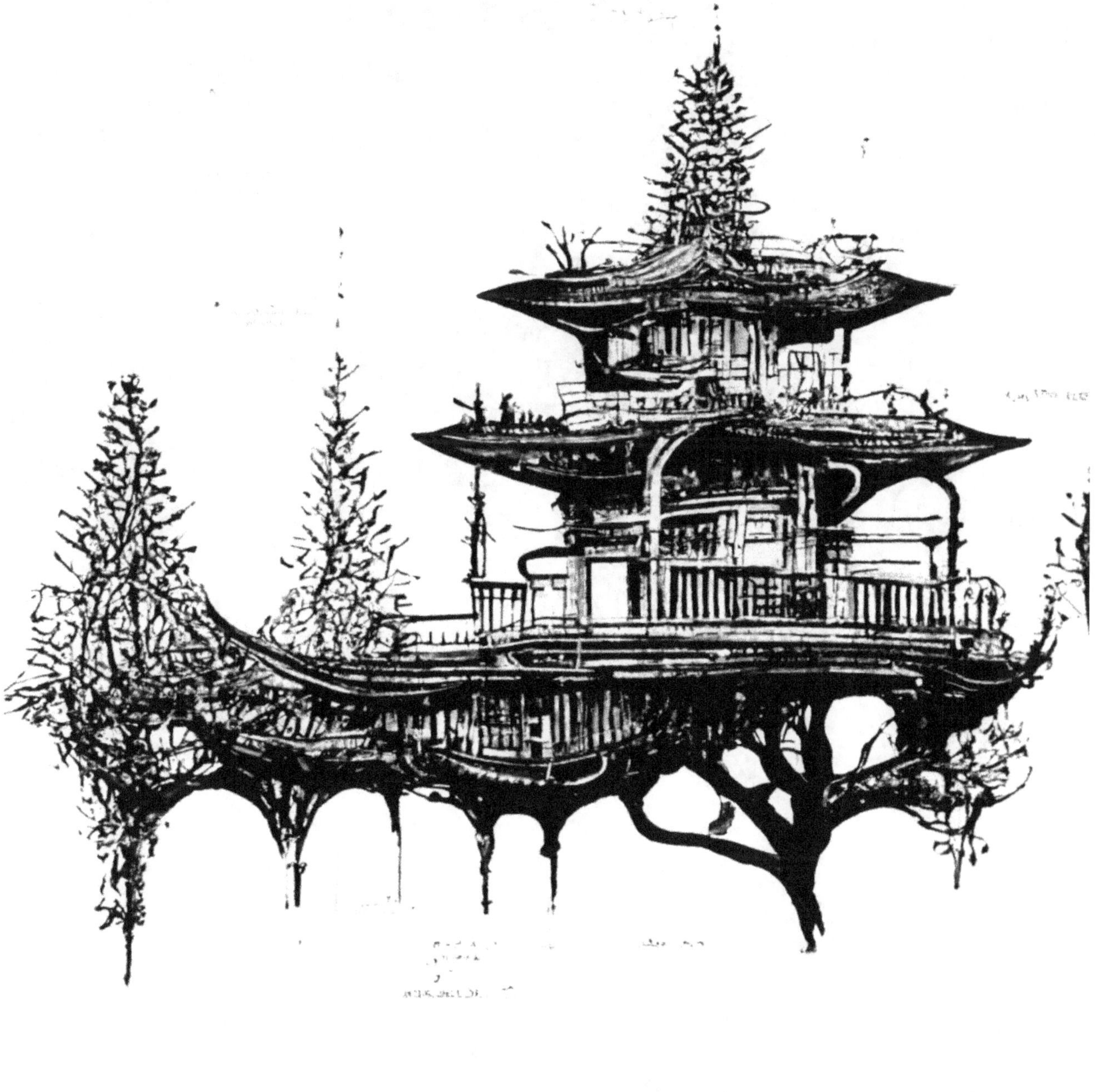

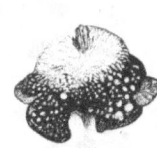
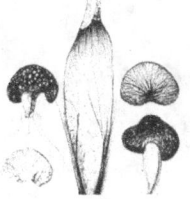

The notes around this house seem to name those responsible for each element, from the house, to the tree design. I really do think the treehouses are completely designed from sapling to maturity.

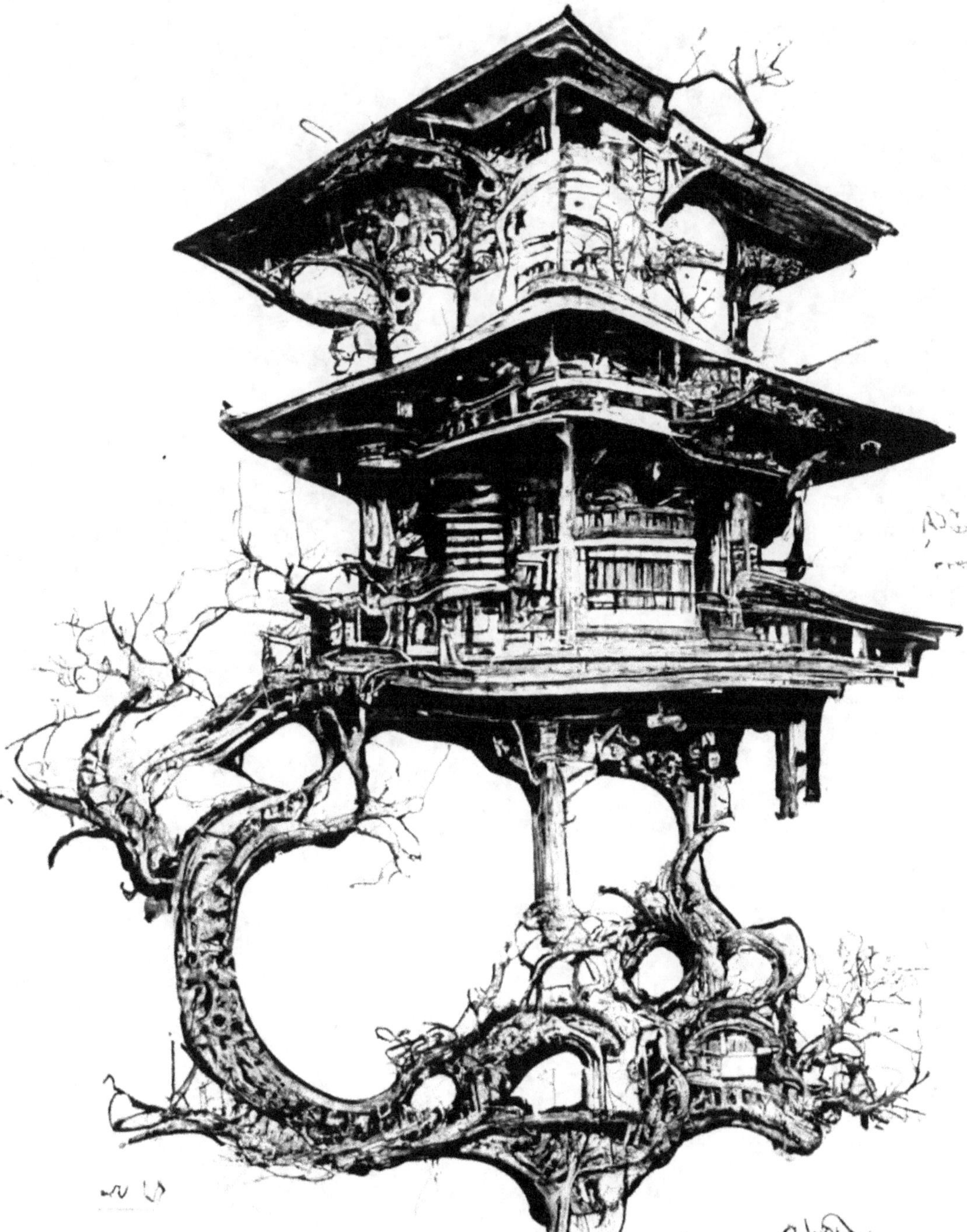

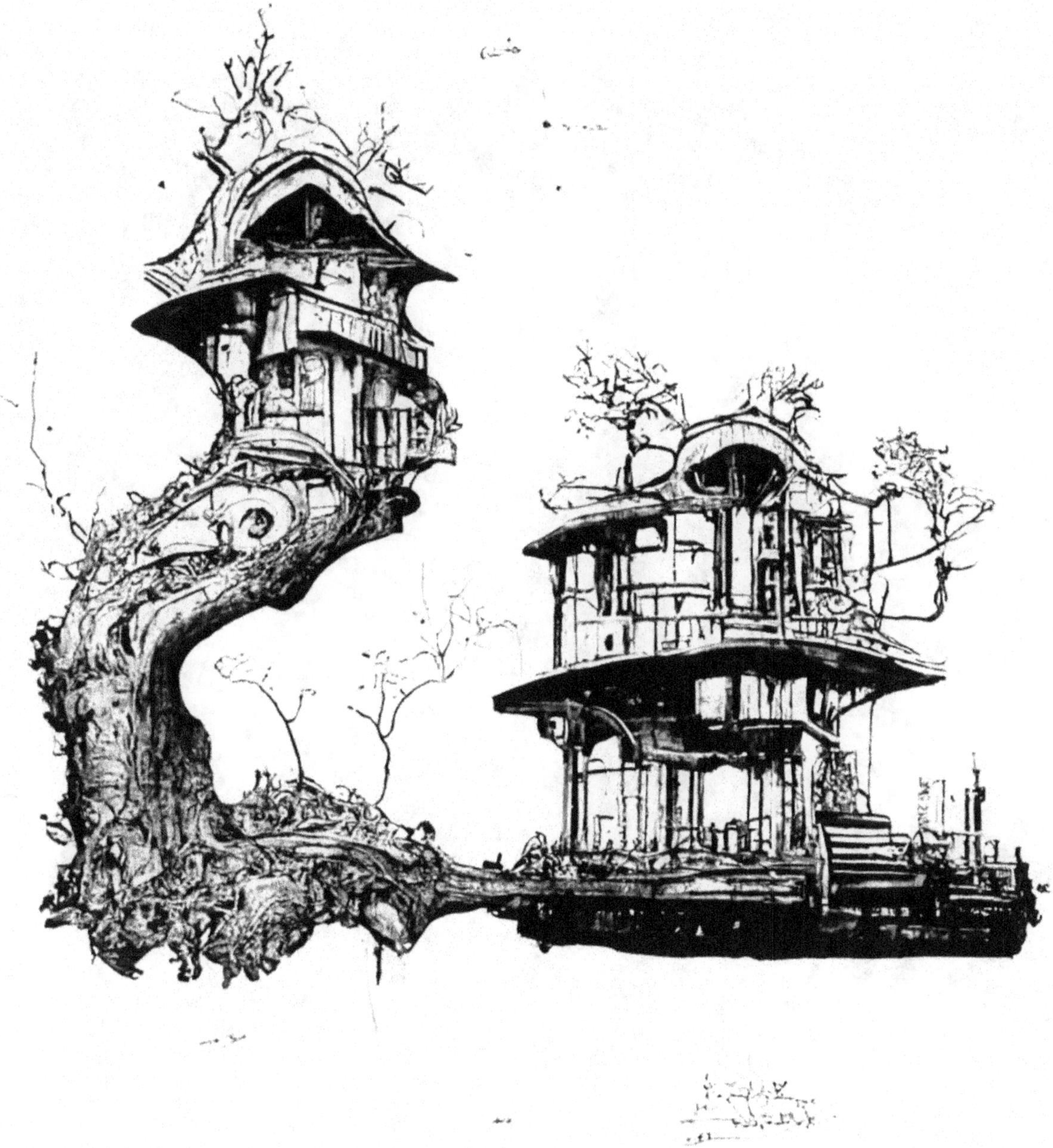

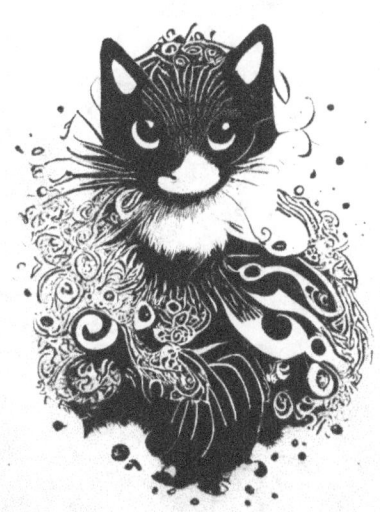

Loosely translated, this is the parental home, and a subsidiary that is intended for a grown child who has not yet married. Much nicer than a basement, don't you think?

An unidentified warrior in the margins speaks to me of the need for offense, as well as the tree houses' indubitable advantages for defense.

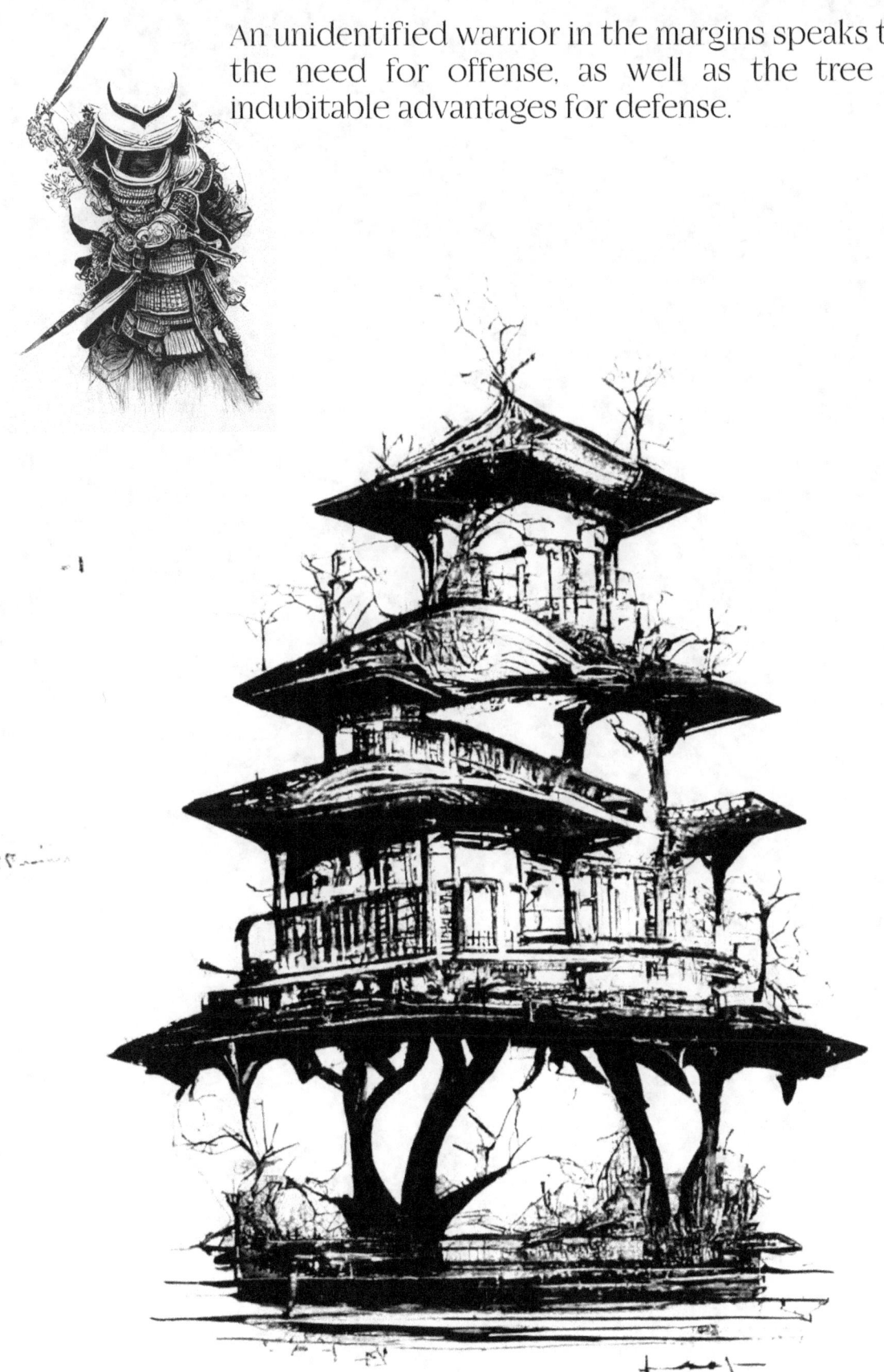

This stilted treehouse is kept in very nice order with branches trimmed, which still allows the supporting trees to live.

These homes often show signs of expanding families, from the additions seemingly added willy-nilly, to the ephemeral rope ladder only a child could love and trust.

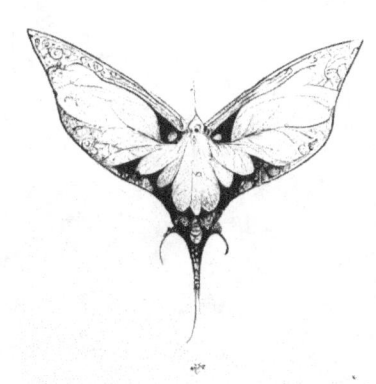

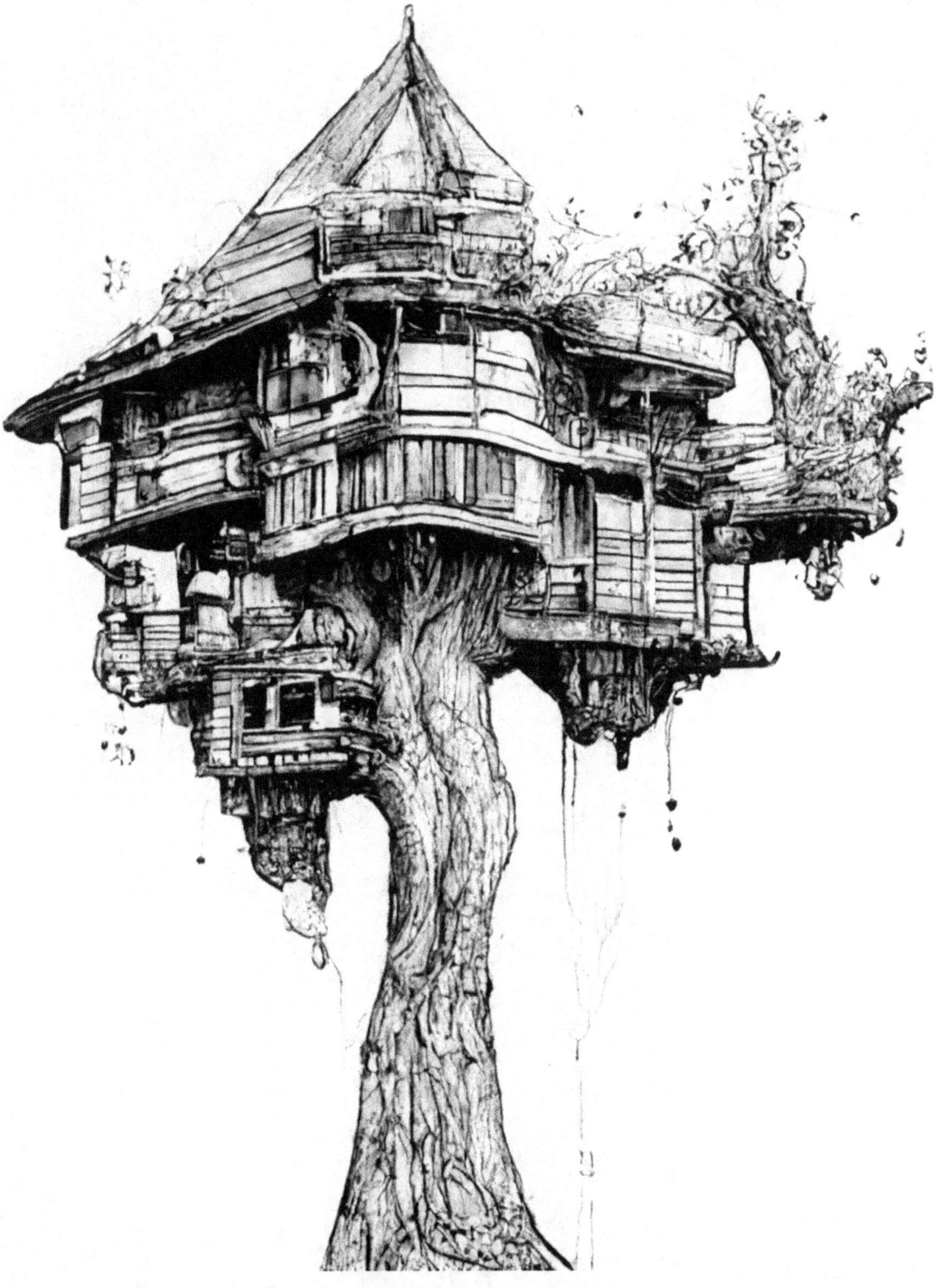

I firmly believe only a winged people could put a kitchen on the top floor of a house with this many spiral staircases.

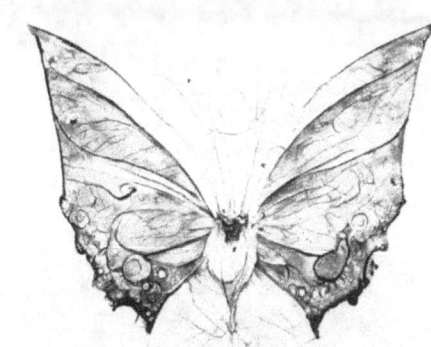

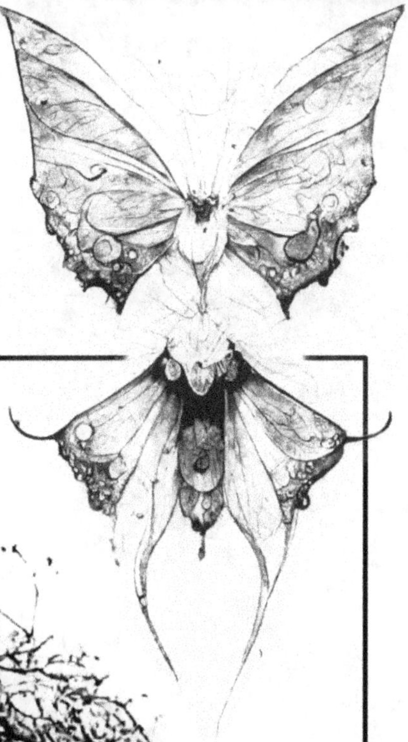

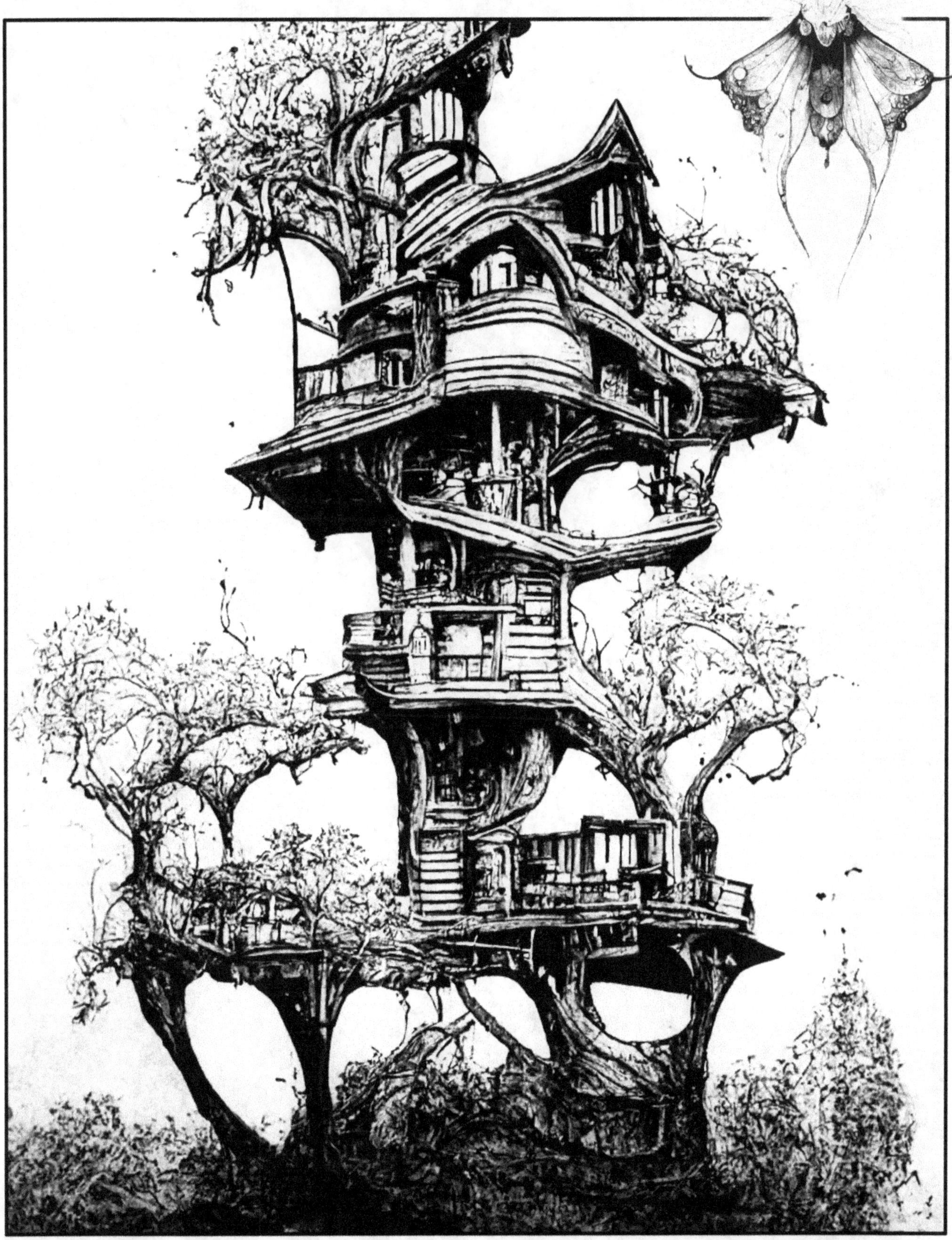

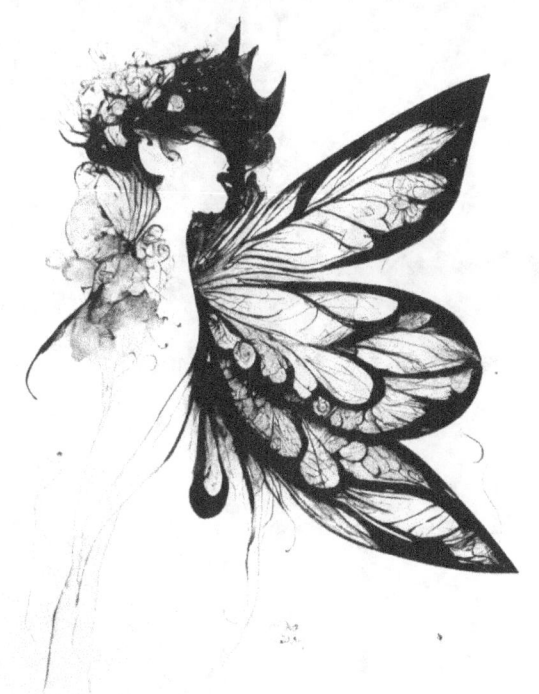

This sketch seems to imply a fairy, or perhaps pixie, but it is sadly incomplete.

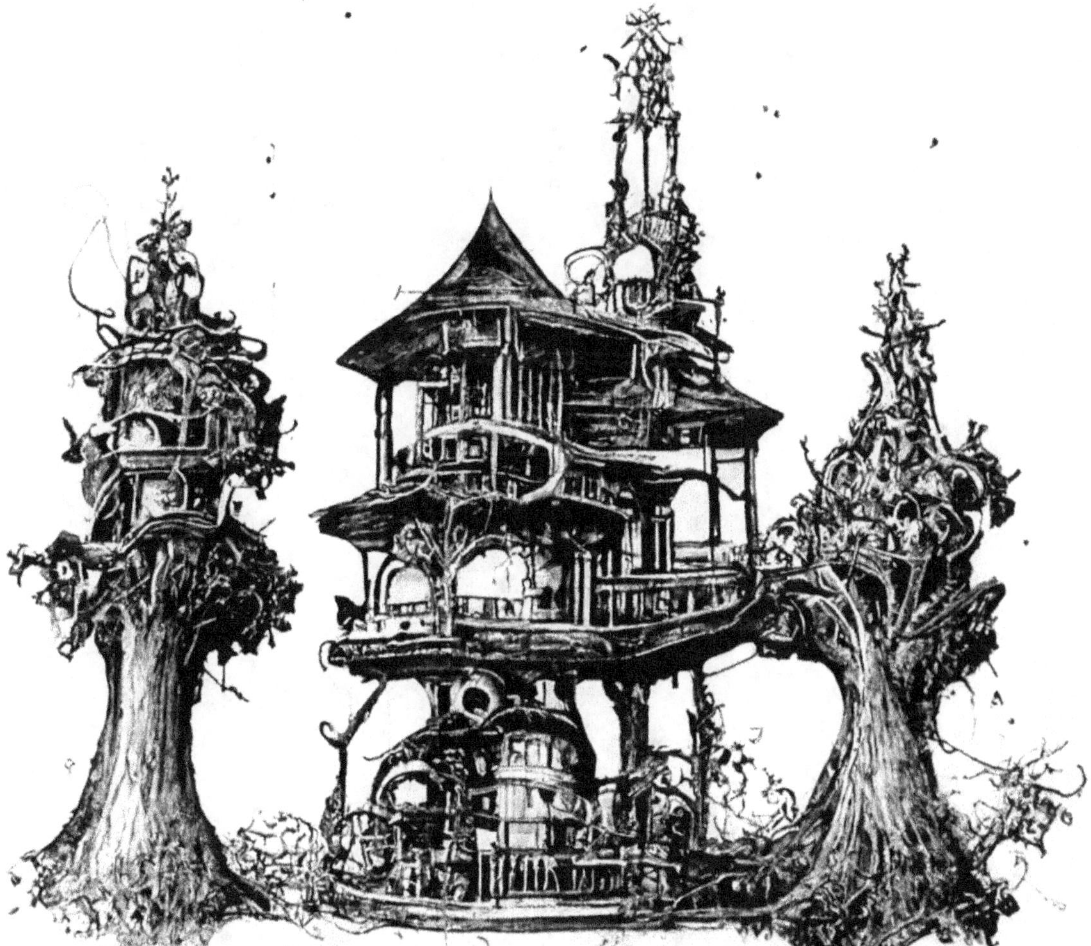

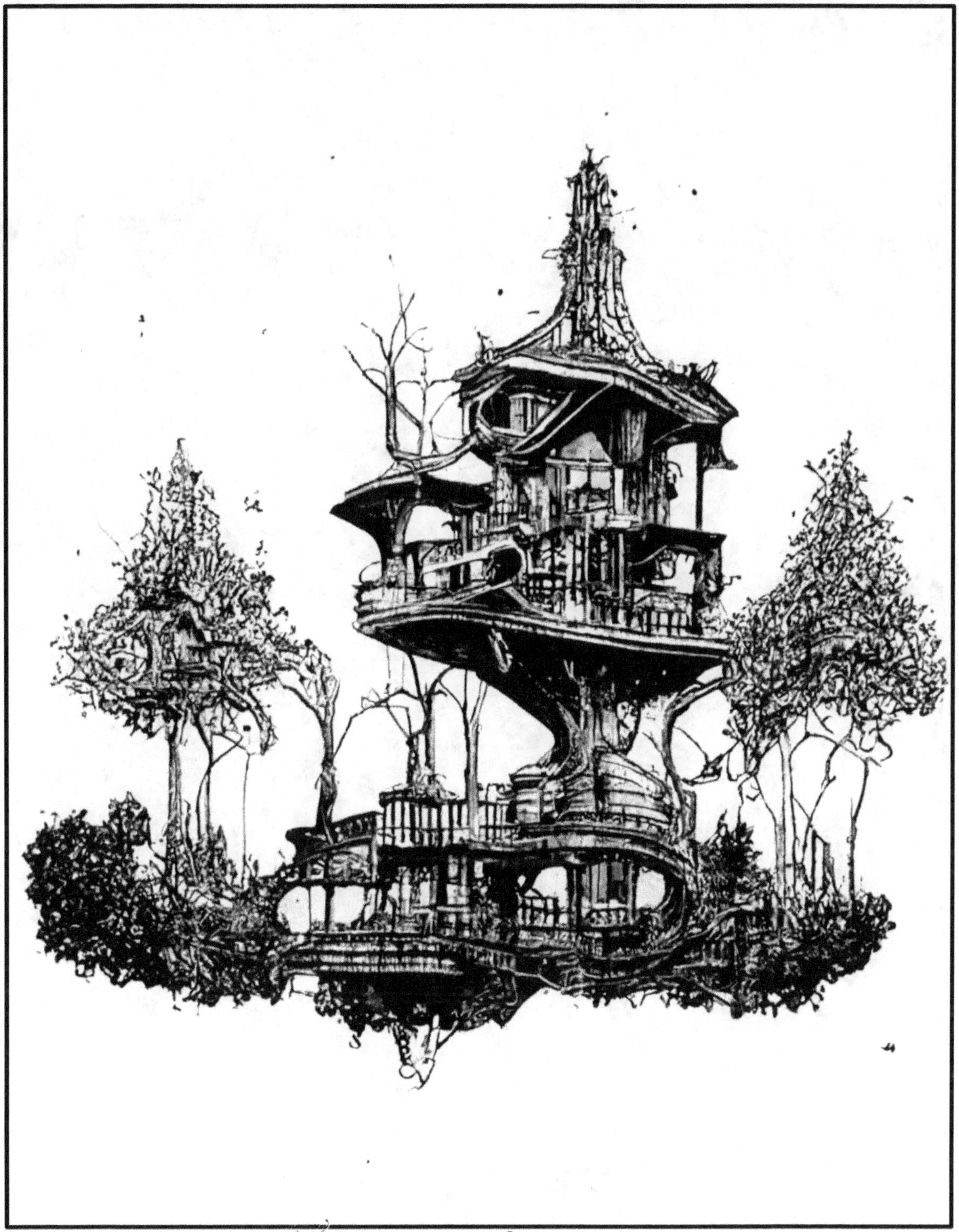

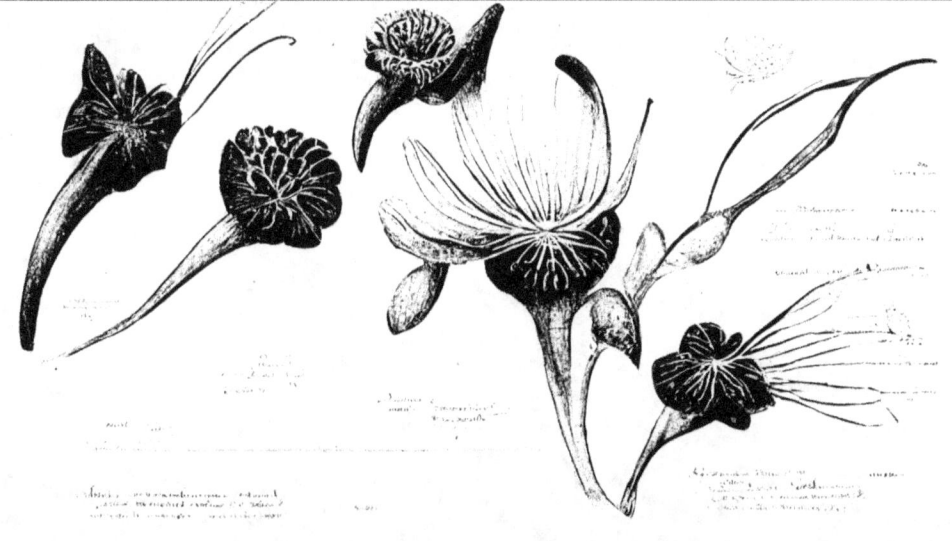

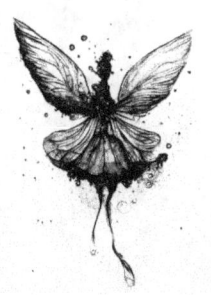 The grand home boasts a setup of pulleys to make travel between floors much easier than steps. The marginalia continue to affirm my assumption of a winged people, but the other species seem not to have wings. Perhaps homes like this serve both?

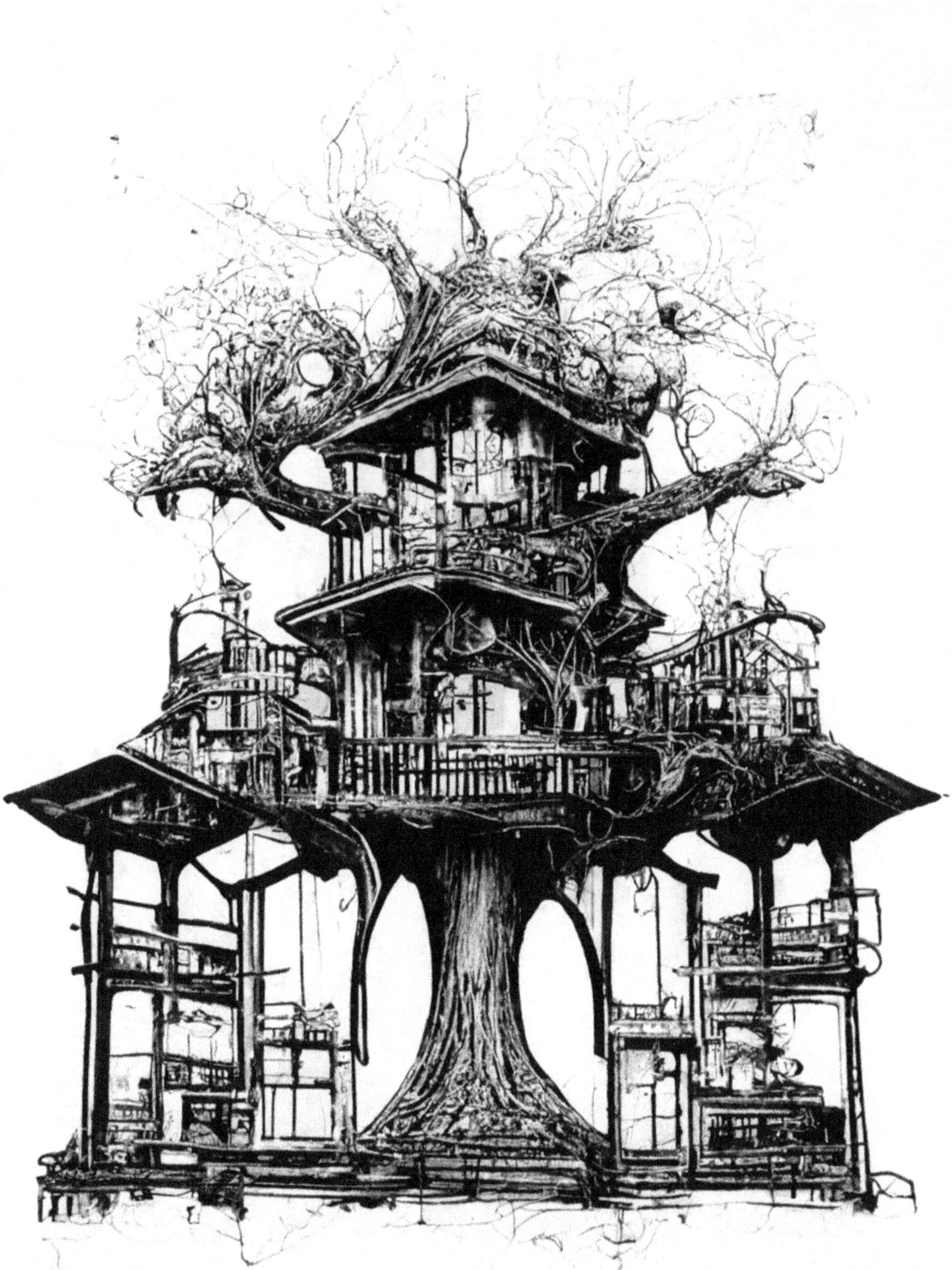

Glimpses of a village from her pages shows me that a uniform style may be ascribed to a region. Still, there is much variance in each dwelling.

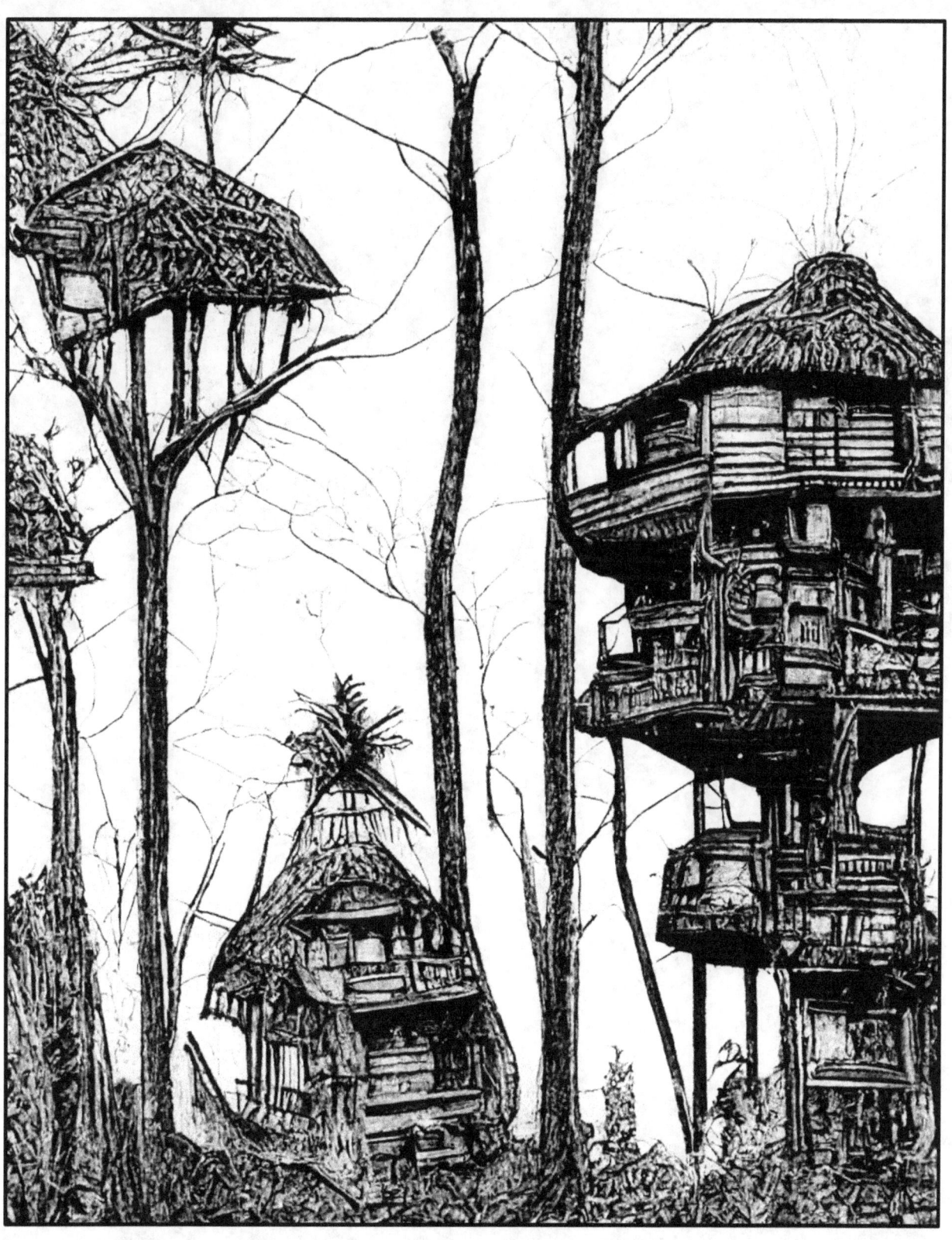

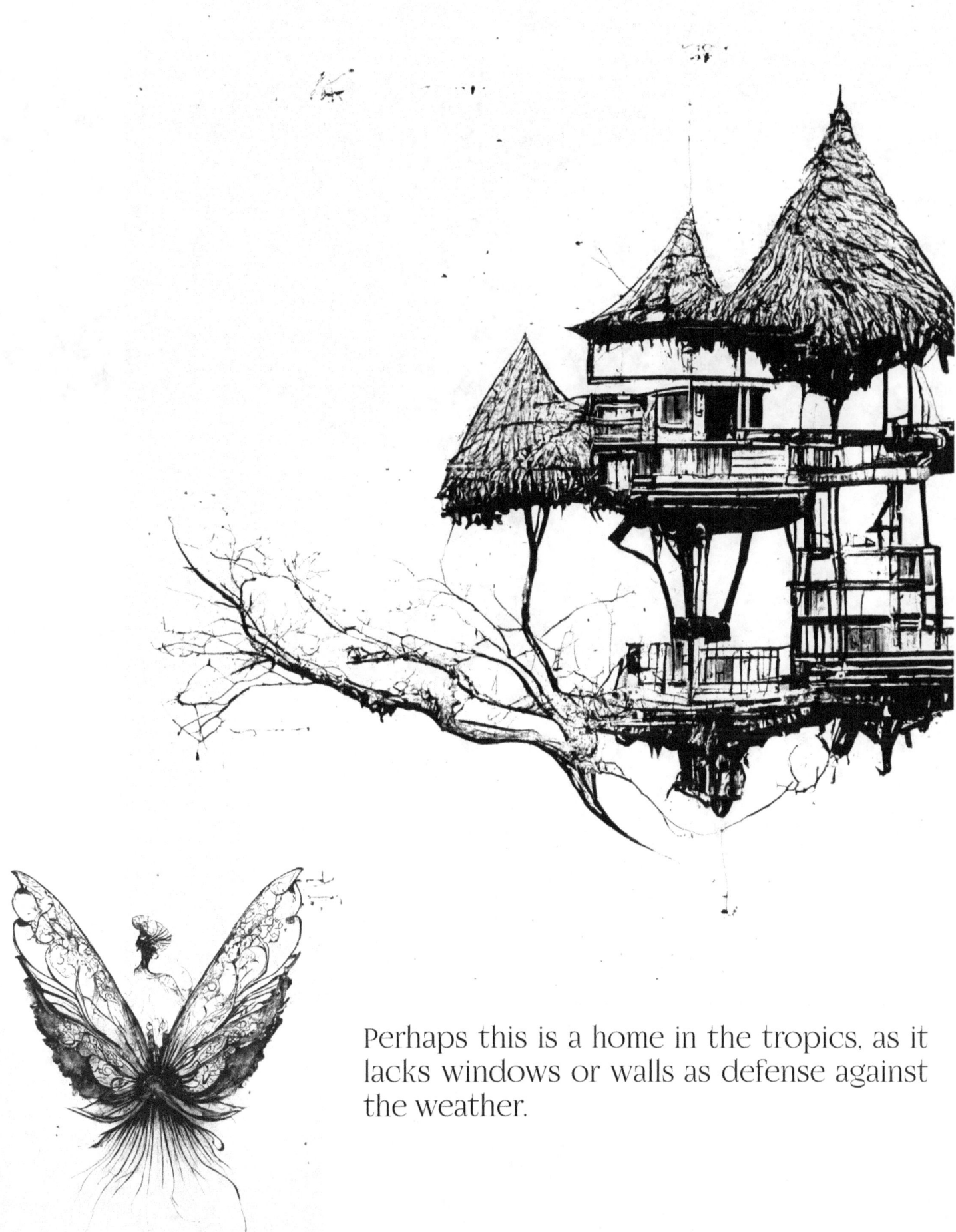

Perhaps this is a home in the tropics, as it lacks windows or walls as defense against the weather.

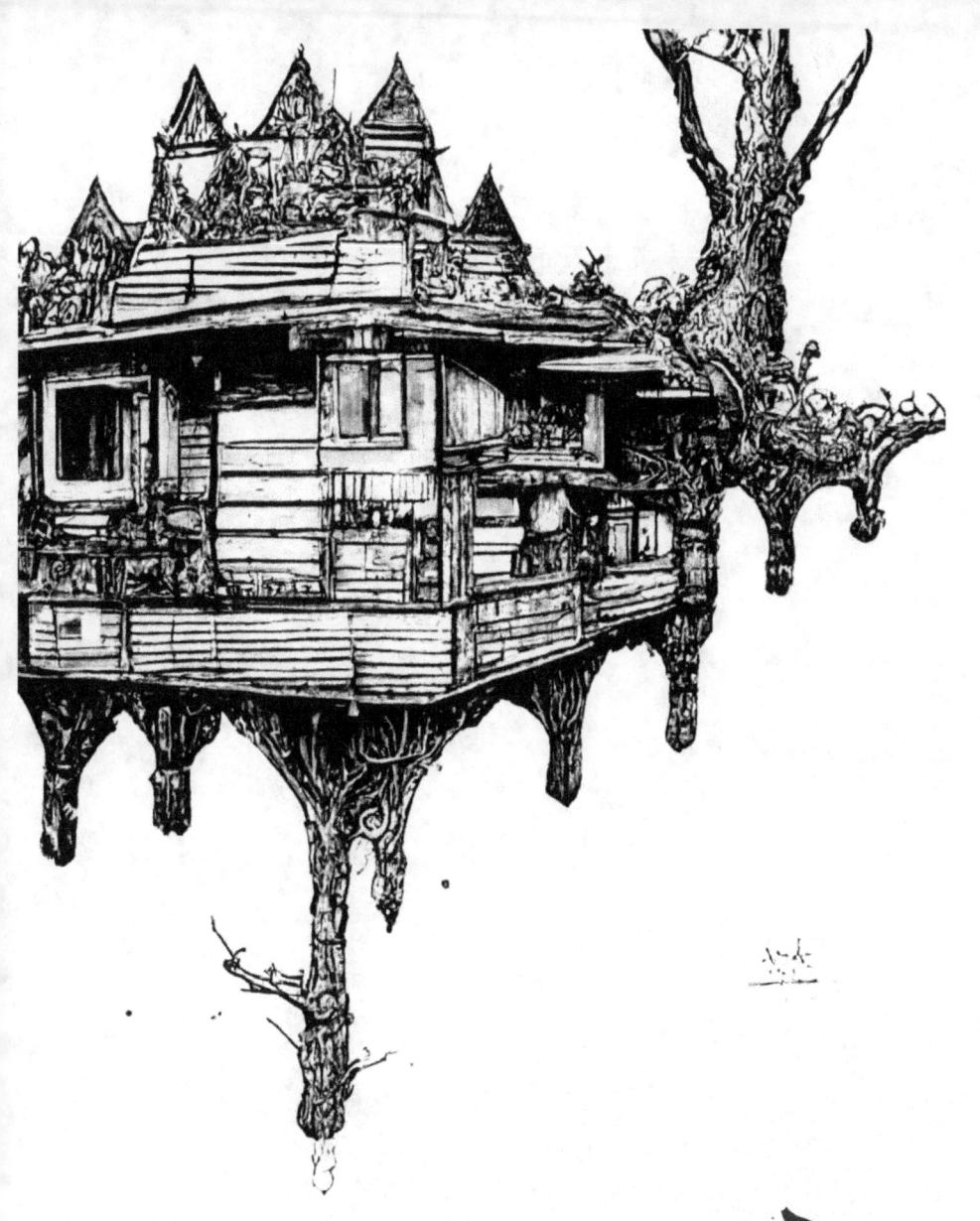

Mme K includes here a brief note, perhaps the name of the place, calling this a Quay House. To my eye it is so much larger than others, it could be an inn.

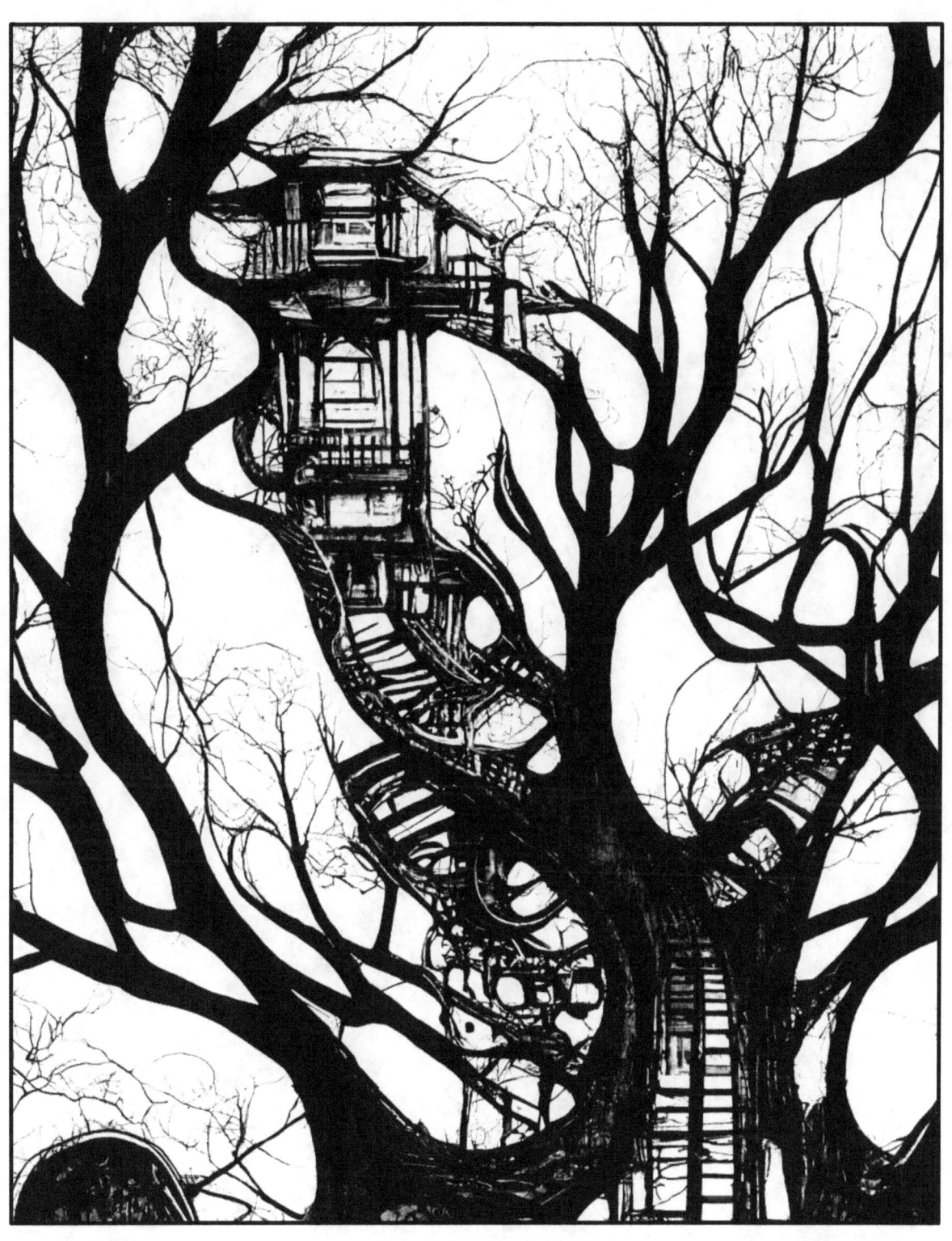

A spiderweb of stairs leads to a tiny house. I wonder why the disproportionate ascent was built?

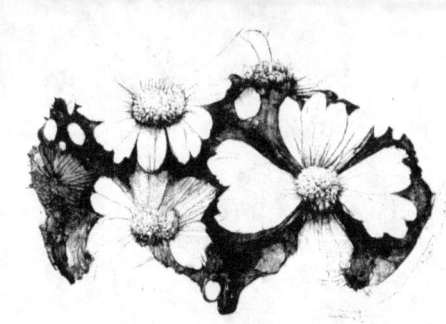

I find the idea of swinging below this home both thrilling and terrifying. It must be a wonderful view when seated there, and if you could not fly, this would be the next best thing so long as you held tight to the ropes!

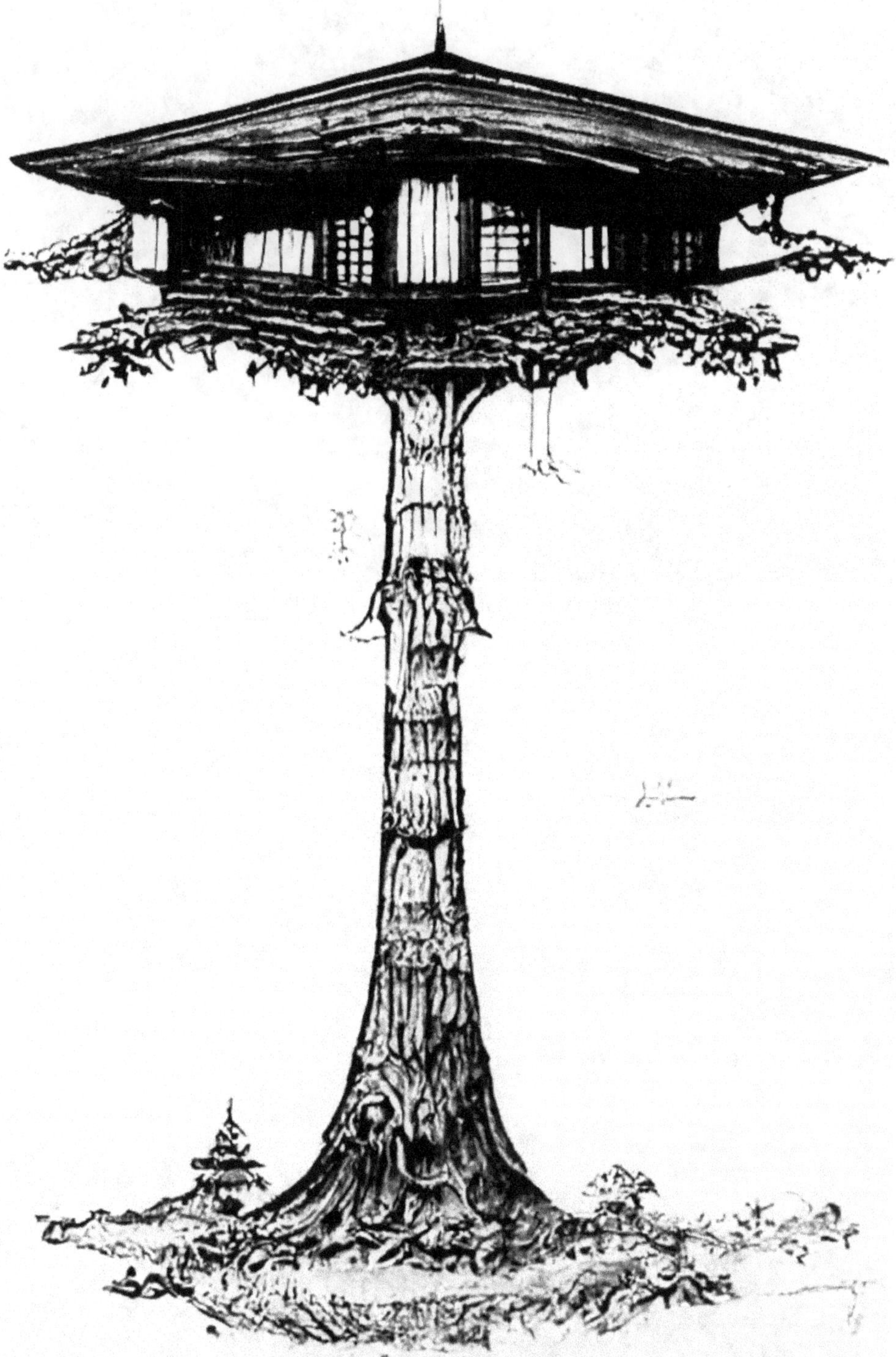

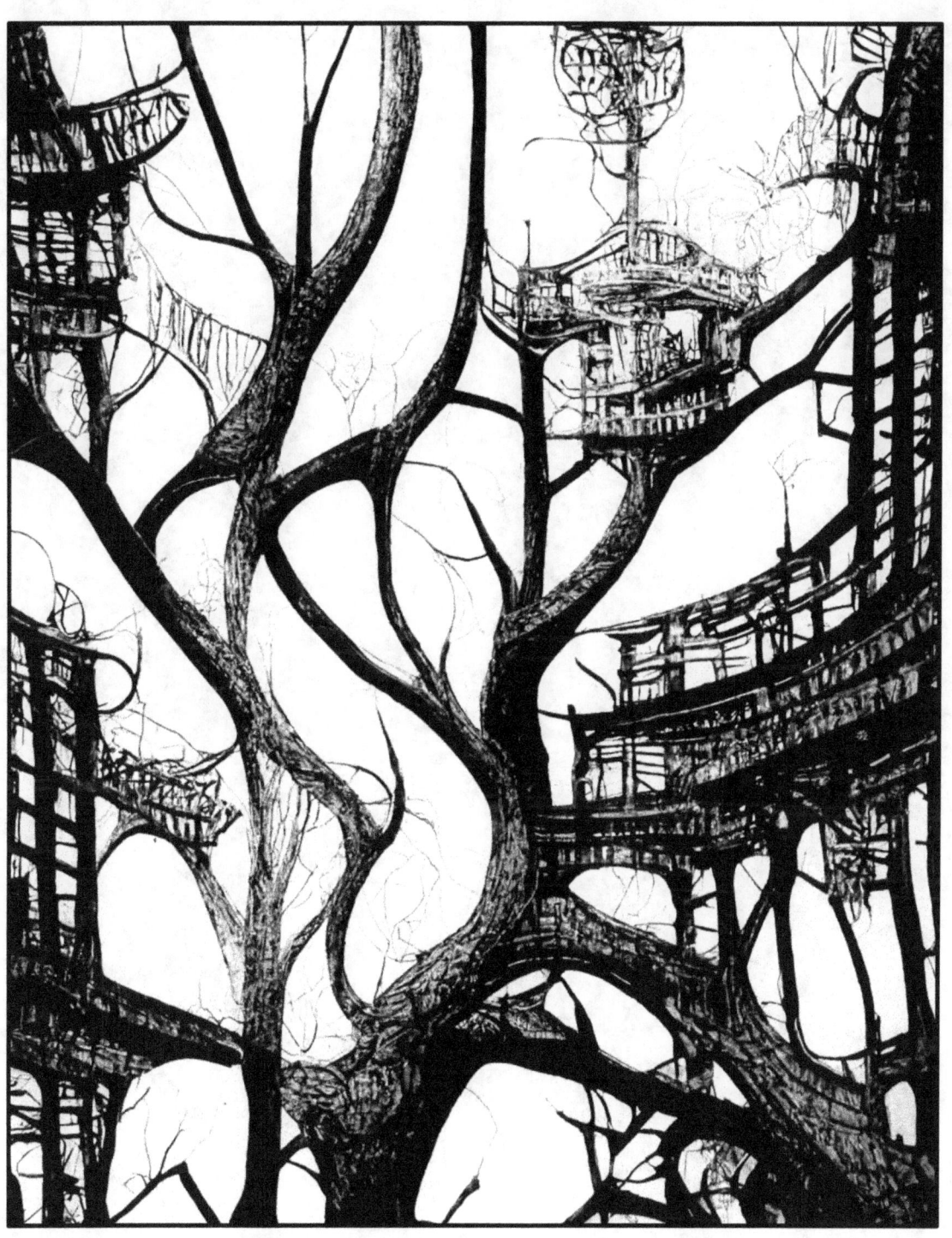
And here we have another peek at a village. Or is it a family compound? Difficult to tell, indeed.

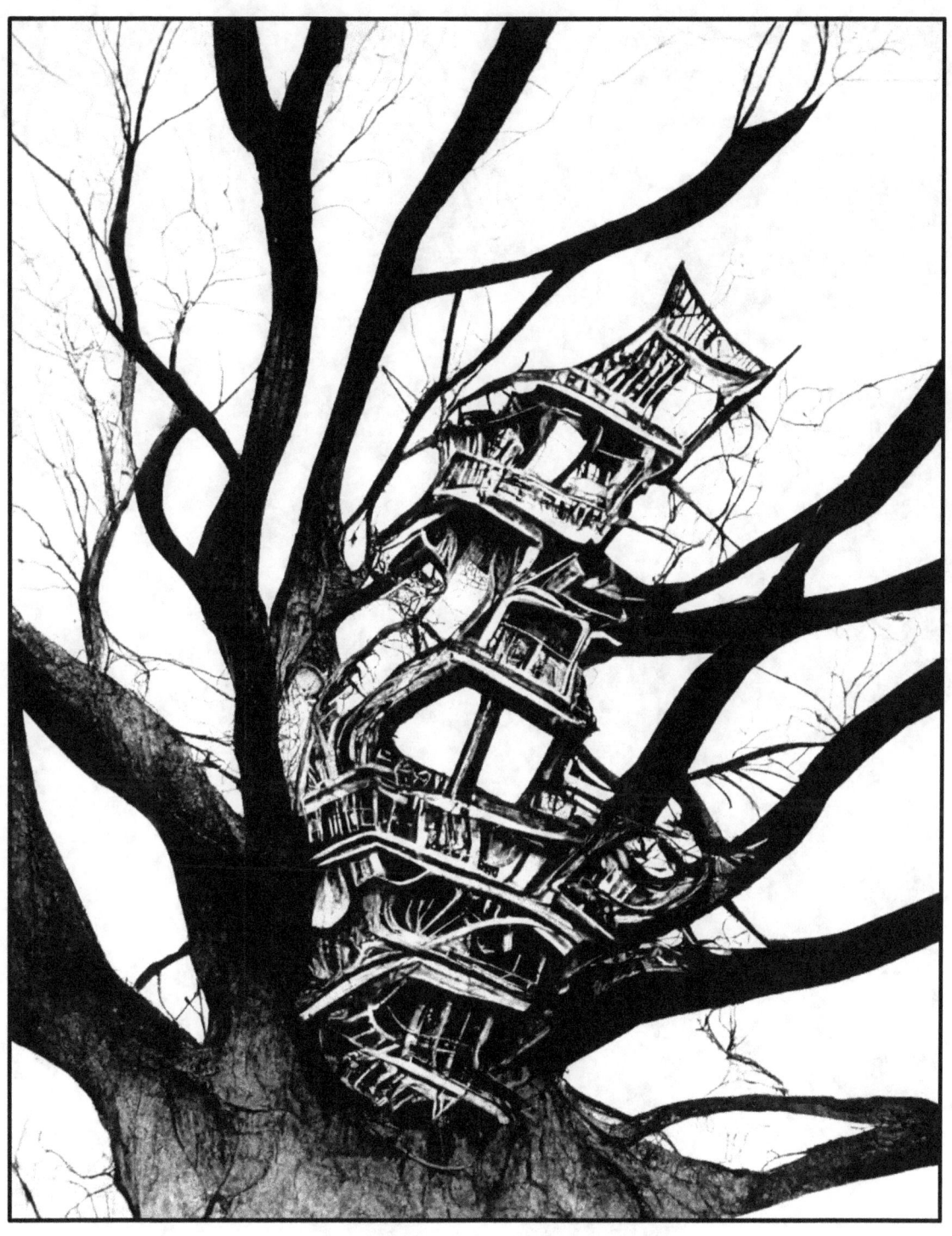

The perspective in this drawing simply must be off. Or the furniture is all at one side of the house in a heap.

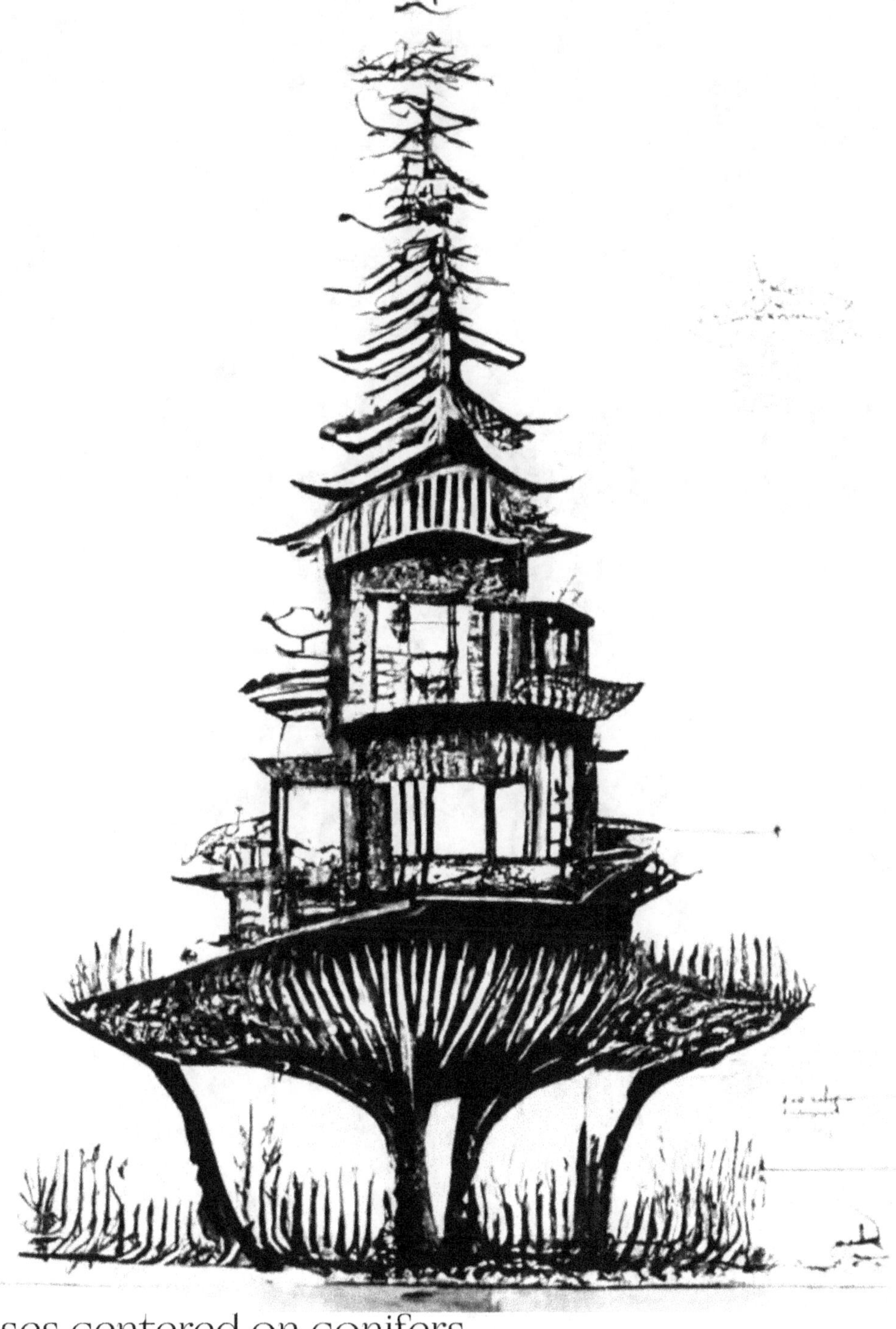

Houses centered on conifers are not commonly shown in her sketches. It is unclear if this represents their overall rarity, or simply that her travels didn't lead her to them.

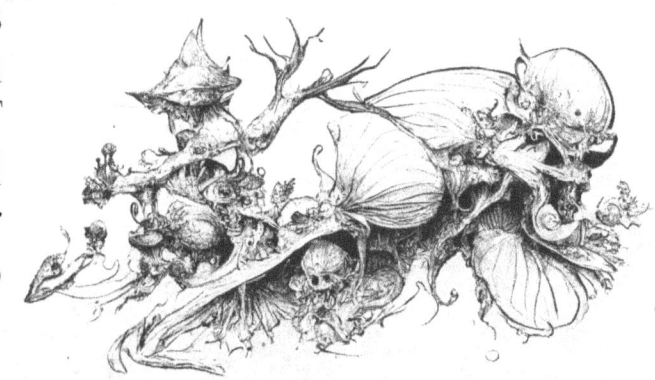

Another of the houses which has been painstakingly designed from warping the living tree, into the final architecture. Just lovely!

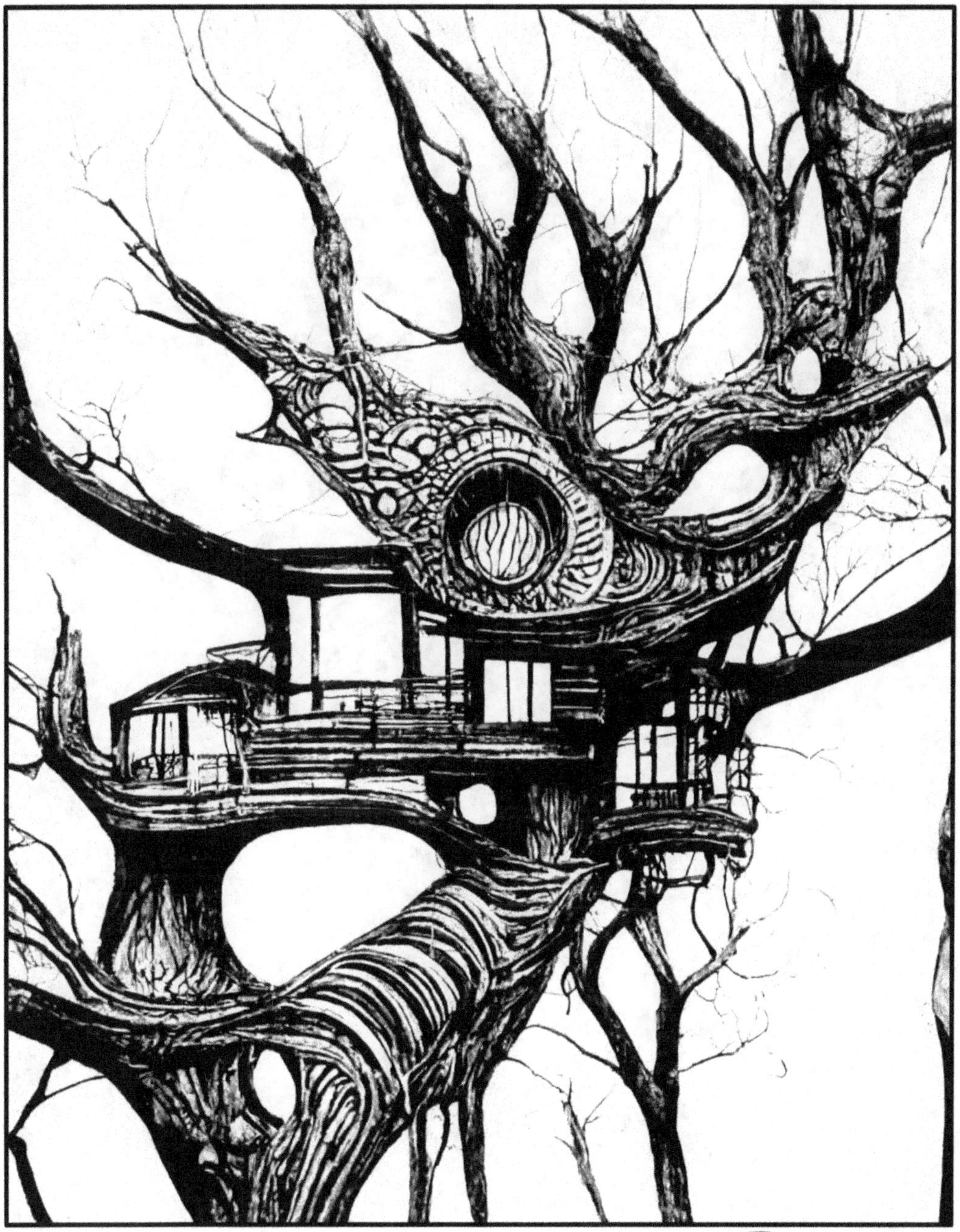

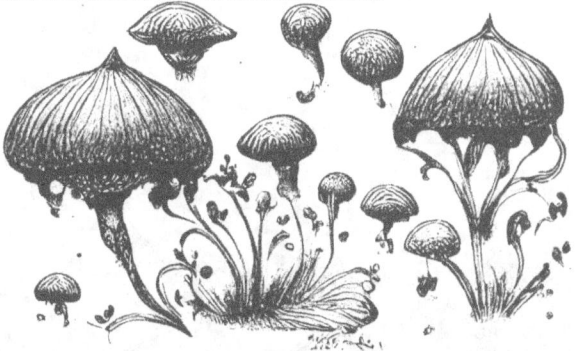

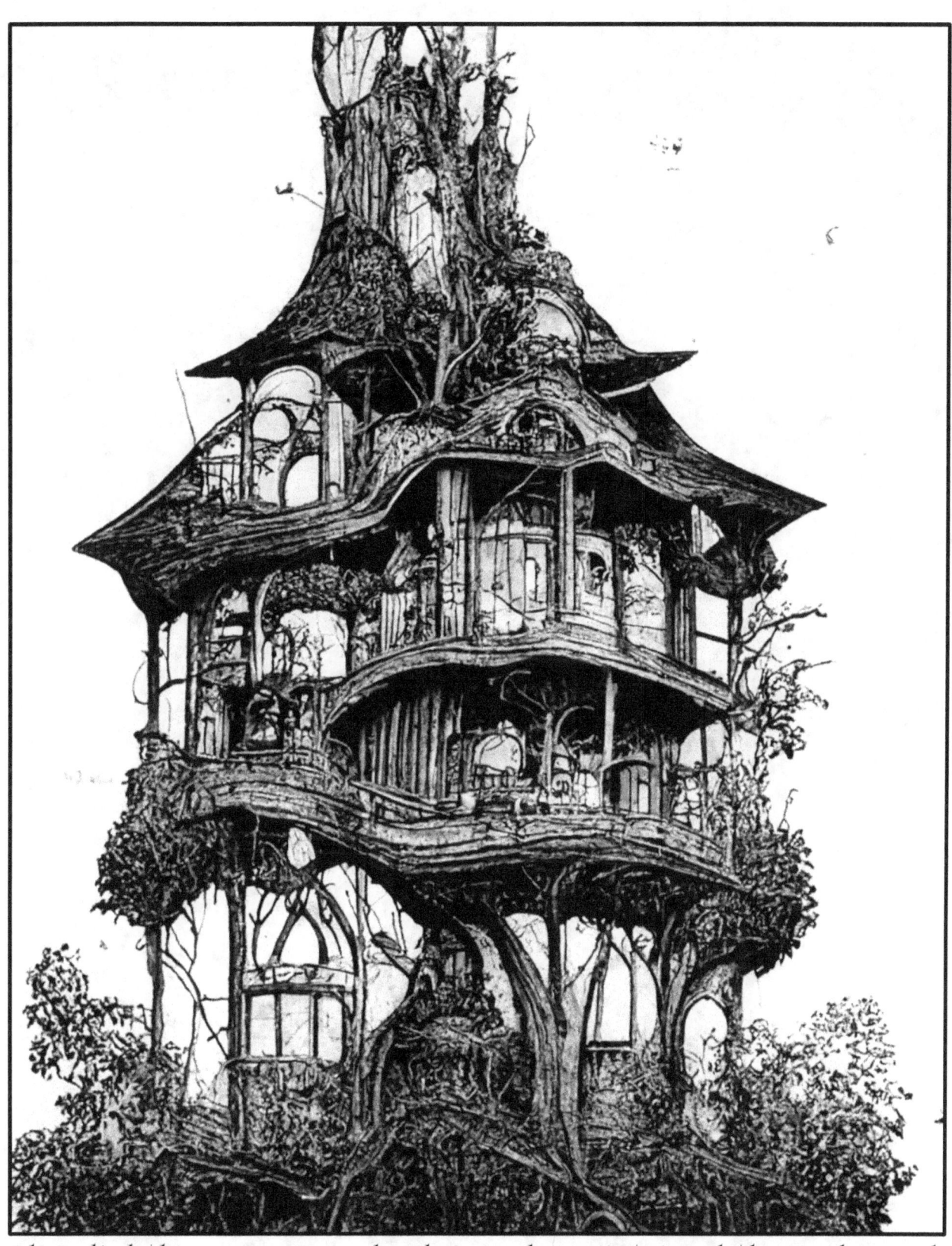
The slightly overgrown look is only maintained through much time and effort, making this house exude a certain appearance of wealth.

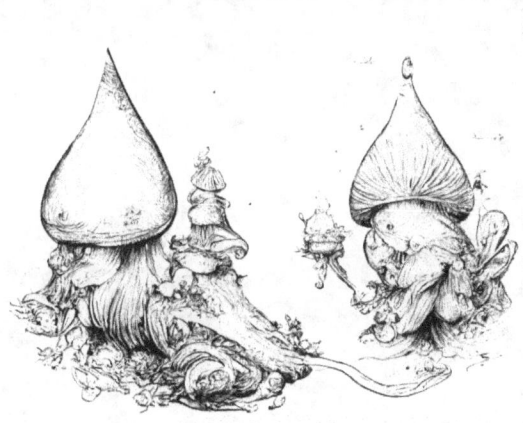

Mme K remarks here on the steep pitch of the roof as being ideal for shedding snow, along with an underground root cellar for climate-controlled food storage.

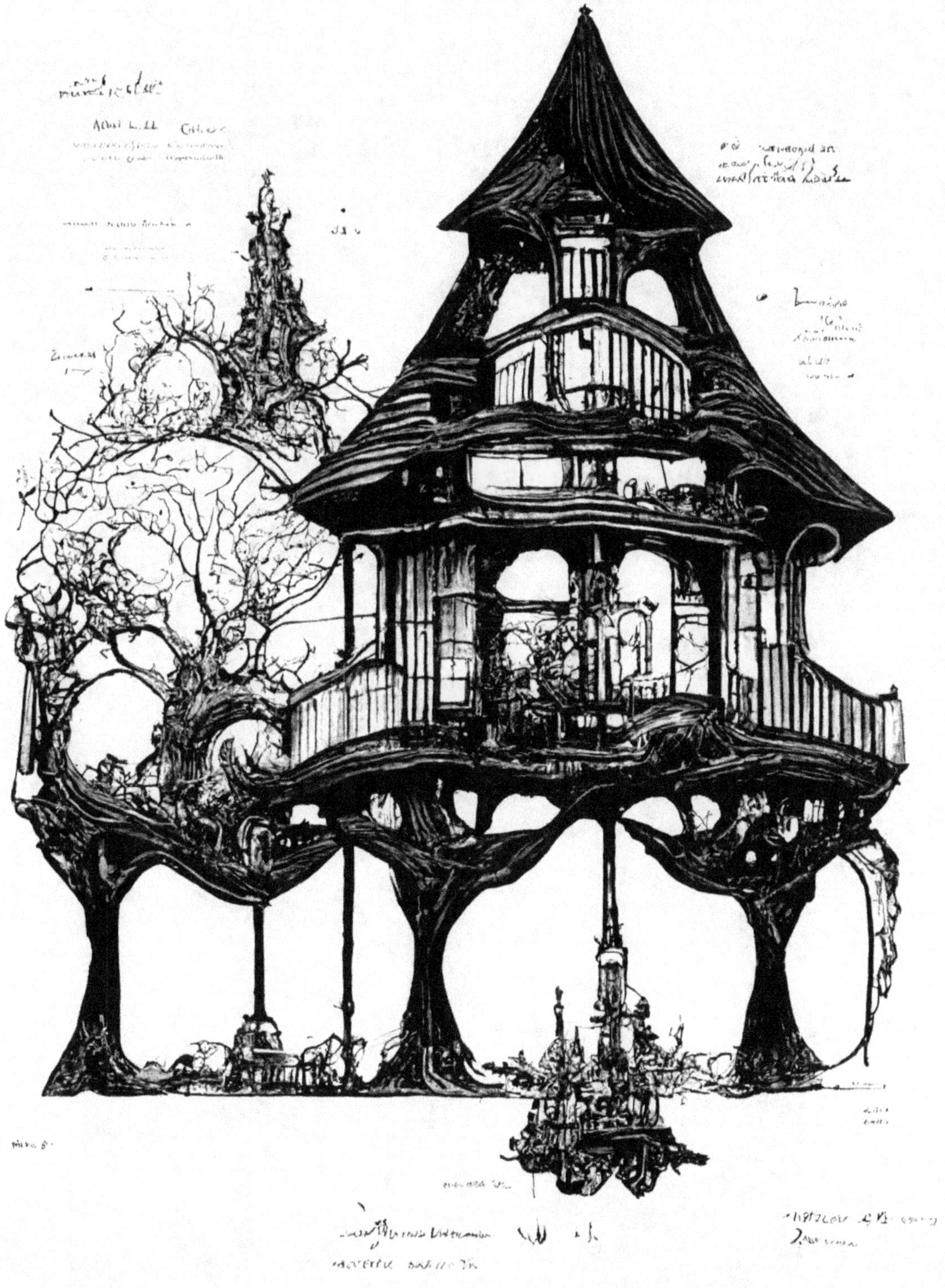

This house is, unusual in her pages, supported on piers, but with plentiful gardens on all levels to sustain the silviculture so important to the peoples of her world.

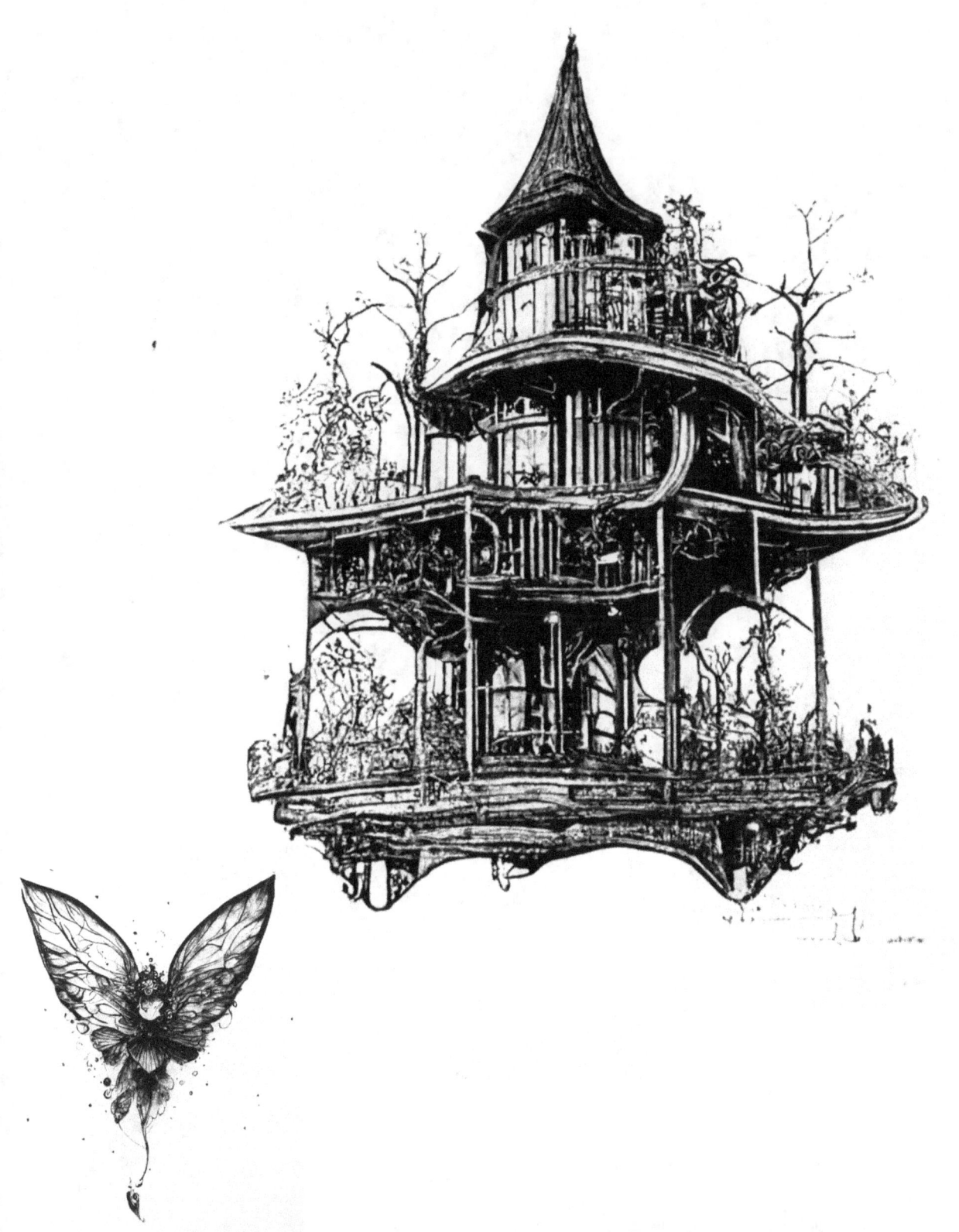

I hope that you enjoyed the pages of Mme K's sketchbook as much as I have. It is truly a glimpse into another world. I am curious to hear if you agree with my deductions about it, from the peoples to the homes and vehicles.

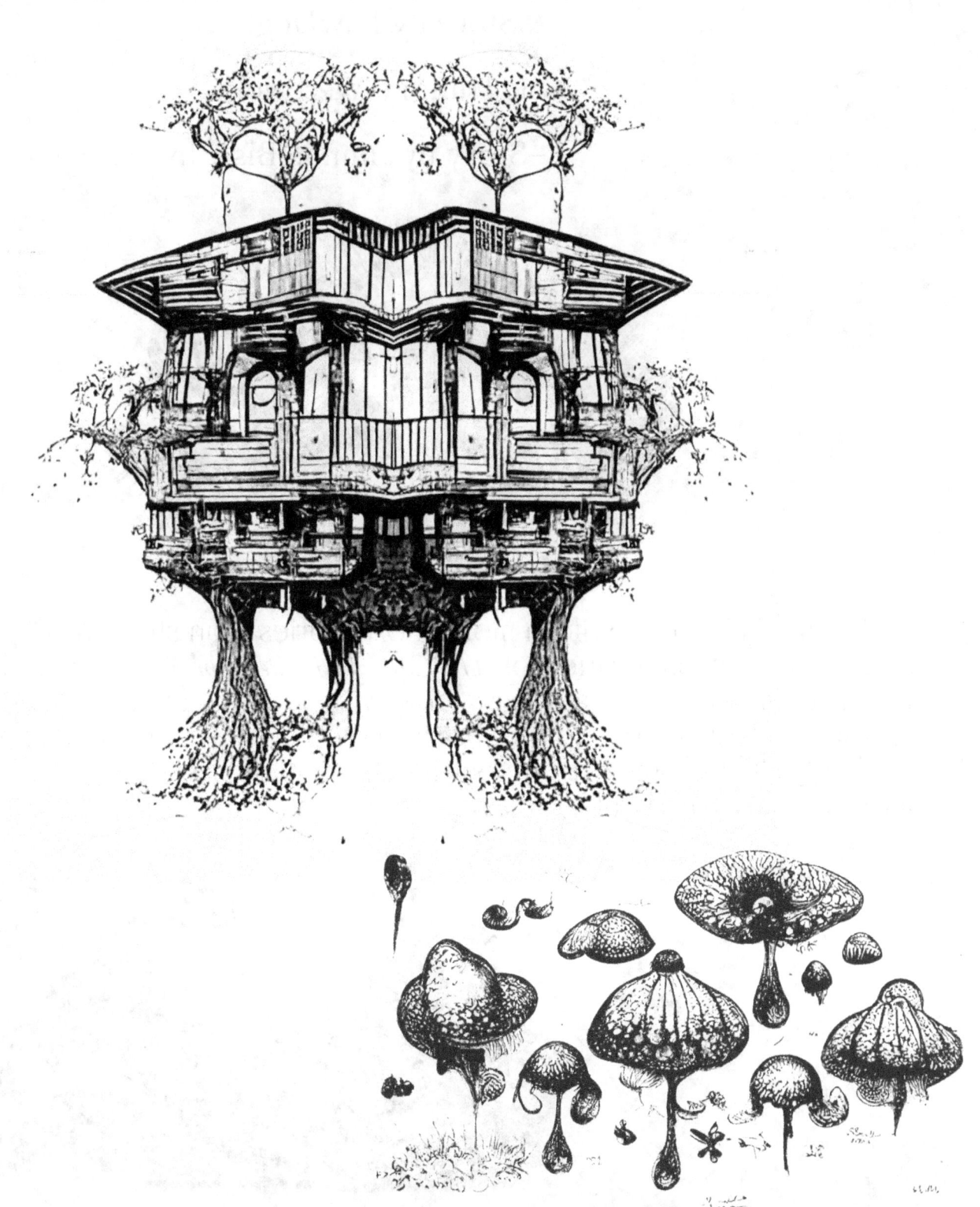

You can find other illustrated books by Cedar Sanderson, including:

Inktail & Friends

Inktail, Too!

The Cute Moose

Taskforce CHIWEENIE and the Poultry Liberation Front

–Story by LawDog

One Hungry Werewolf

–Story by Jimmie Bise, Jr

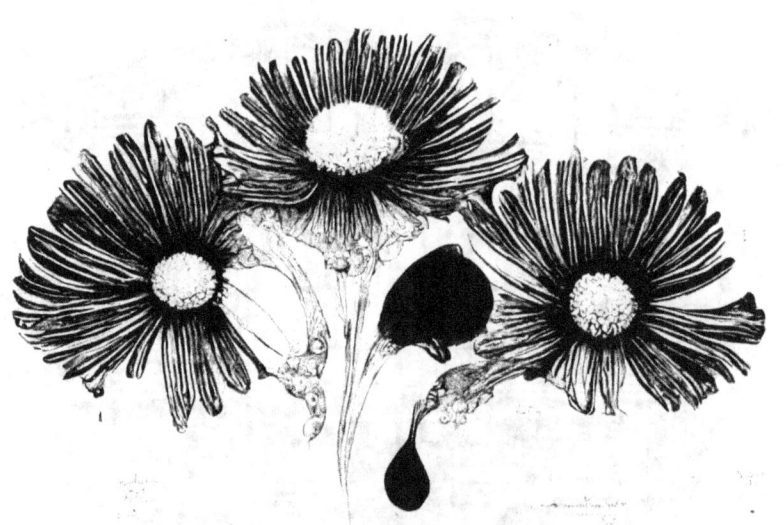

Cedar Sanderson has written more short stories than she can keep track of, and the recent publication of *The Case of the Perambulating Hatrack* makes her tenth novel in print. She also has a blog with over a decade of essays, recipes, and artwork for you to explore should you so desire at www.cedarwrites.com. Currently she lives in north Texas with a patient First Reader, a dog, a cat, and a teenager to round out the menagerie.

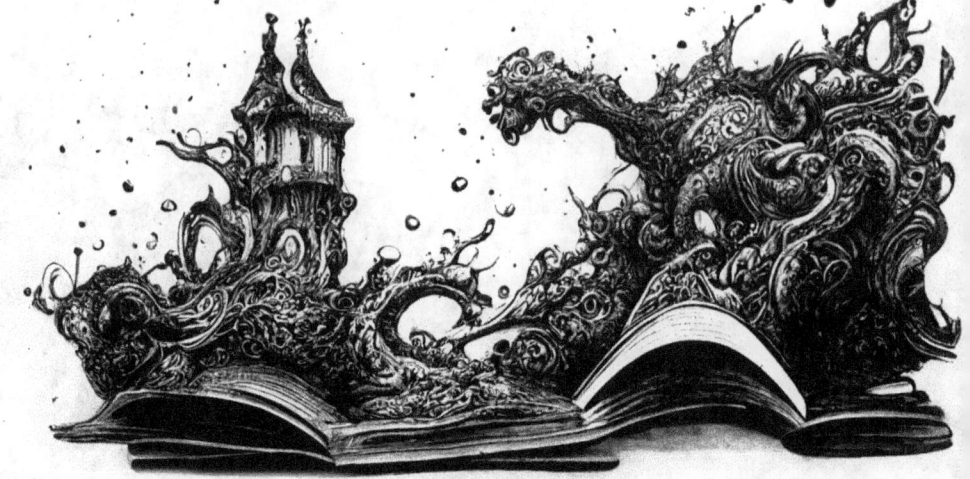

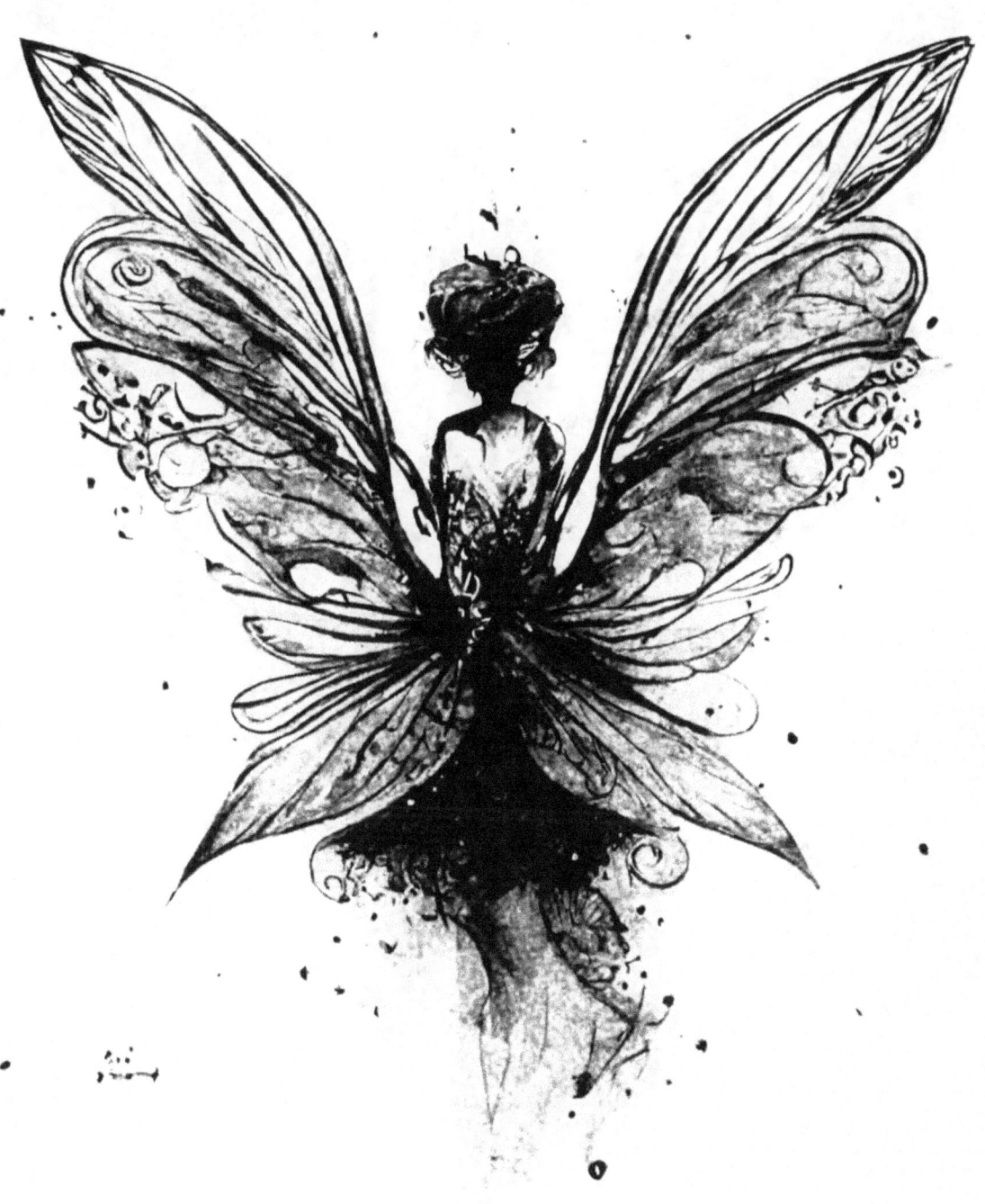

www.ingramcontent.com/pod-product-compliance
Lightning Source LLC
Chambersburg PA
CBHW080501220526
45465CB00006B/2345